Sowerby Tales

Jean Illingworth

Best Wishes,
Jean Illingworth

Published by Royd House
The Book Case
29 Market Street
Hebden Bridge
West Yorks.
HX7 6EU
www.bookcase.co.uk

© Jean Illingworth, 2011
Front cover photo: View of Sowerby from Stanhope, © Malcolm Street
Back cover picture: Painting by Beryl Waddington based on a photograph of
Town Gate taken from the top of the church tower by Thomas Heap, c.1913.
Back cover photograph of Jean Illingworth: Conner Photography

Cover design: Kate Claughan

We have made all reasonable efforts to ensure that the reproduction of
all content on these pages is done with the consent of copyright owners
and any errors or omissions are unintentional.

ISBN: 978-1-907197-07-9

SOWERBY: THE REAL YORKSHIRE

FOREWORD BY AUSTIN MITCHELL

Sowerby isn't one of those romantic, rural villages where ploughmen homeward plod their weary way, Miss Marple tends the flowers and bodies pile up in some Midsomer morgue with a thatched roof. All that's in the spoiled South. Sowerby is in the real world of the North, on the hills of the Calder Valley. There hill farmers scratch a living rather than count the money flowing in from the Common Agricultural Policy, life is harder, the people tougher and, being Yorkshire folk, terser. It's the real world of hard lives and millstone grit, houses and people.

Which makes the Sowerby story as well worth telling as Akenfield's, but more important to the country, for it was hill villages like Sowerby which started the industrial revolution before it moved down into the valleys to make Yorkshire the wool capital of the world and Britain an industrial, not an agricultural, society. Sowerby's story and that of its people deserve to be told. Now, thanks to Calderdale's own Studs Terkel, Jean Illingworth, Sowerby's has been. Here it is.

Sowerby is a small canvas to paint. Today it's a couple of thousand people living in what used to be Council houses, or in the old millstone grit houses and the halls out on the hills. Yet in Saxon times it was the ancient centre of the whole area, and long remained far more important than its offspring, Sowerby Bridge, down in the valley. Sowerby was the capital of the Anglo Saxon Sowerby Shire and remained more important than its little brother right up to the late nineteenth century.

I mustn't bore you with my enthusiasm for history, for in fact the Sowerby story really begins in the seventeenth century when the profits of the land and wool merchanting endowed the area with the splendid Jacobean halls and houses which still adorn it: Wood Lane Hall, Haugh End, Old Field House, Sowerby Hall, White Windows and others, building up to the magnificent Field House (1749) and its dower house, Longfield (1728), in the eighteenth century. All these proud halls and some of the houses in Sowerby are adorned with the dates and initials of the owners, the first wool barons. Foremost among them were the Stansfelds who swiped the stone of the old church to use at Field House when they endowed Sowerby with its magnificent parish church, built in 1762 at a cost of £2,909-12s-9d, with a majesty and style out of all proportion to the little village clustered round it.

Sowerby's main street housed shops, estate workers and handloom weavers working on the putting out system doing their own spinning, weaving, fulling and dyeing, then despatching their products to Halifax to be sold in the Piece Hall. Sowerby was the kind of village (and may indeed have been the actual village) Daniel Defoe described when he made his descent from his traumatic passage over Blackstone Edge to Halifax. Here was the start of the industrial revolution but the next stage of that revolution, with water, then steam power and the new machinery for spinning and weaving, moved the centre of gravity down from Sowerby to Sowerby Bridge. There the woollen mills and the textile engineering industry flourished in the nineteenth century, providing the jobs which the population of Sowerby, abandoning handloom weaving, worked at.

Sowerby declined. The population of its local government district fell from 3,653 in 1901 to 3,180 in 1921 and after that it ceased to be counted as a separate area, merely as part of the total of 20,558 (1931) population of Sowerby Bridge. Sowerby Bridge had grown into a typical, and prosperous, mill town but Sowerby village, dominated still by the rich land-owning gentry families, the Stansfelds and the Rawsons, carried on in its old settled ways into a slow decline with an earlier way of life still preserved.

Which brings us to the twentieth century, the period so well chronicled by Jean Illingworth. Sowerby began the century as a self-contained, small, community with its own churches and chapels, a Co-op Store, a butchery, its own Post Office and schools. It was a good place to live until the last decades of the century saw rapid change and an industrial decline which changed Sowerby from an independent community living apart, to a periphery, almost a poor suburb, of Sowerby Bridge. That process of drift to the towns was going on everywhere. It had a bigger impact in Sowerby because by the 1970s the whole area, of which Sowerby was a part, was itself in decline as the wool industry died.

It was decline all round as both hill farming and the job market became tougher. It hit Sowerby just after several years of population increase as Sowerby Bridge Council cleared the most deprived parts of the industrial slums in the valley and moved the residents up the hill to fresh air, and the new Council estates, first in Beechwood, just before and after the Second World War, then in the Newlands after it. That growth destroyed half the village as the old houses on the left hand side of Main Street were pulled down in the "search and destroy" housing renewal policy which prevailed in those days. It was nothing less than Council vandalism. Mercifully, it was stopped before it moved on to demolish Millbank but it left Sowerby lopsided: older houses on the right, Council estate to the left.

At the same time the props of the old society were collapsing. The chapels closed and were eventually pulled down; the Methodists, Baptists and Congregationalists all fell victim to declining congregations, leaving only the magnificent parish church of St Peter's, its majesty slowly decaying, and Steep Lane Baptist which had to lose a storey at heavy cost because of decay. This loss of churches was a double blow because up to the advent of the cinema (Sowerby didn't have one) and the television (everyone had one), the churches had a crucial social role as community centres, youth clubs and music and entertainment centres. As they declined Sowerby found itself bereft of all such facilities. Sowerby Bridge and further-away Halifax were the only alternatives but there entertainment and social facilities were commercial and more expensive. More important, Sowerby's economic underpinning of jobs in textiles and engineering collapsed, destroyed by the de-industrialisation and economic decline which closed all the mills, with Eddleston's the last to go. This destroyed the jobs and left the whole area poorer, its people dependent on benefits, public services and casual jobbing. It was a sad reversal of the growth and contentment which had gone on since the sixteenth century.

The gentry families died out, Major Stansfeld died in 1964. His wife lived on at Field House. When I moved in next door, Mrs. Stansfeld was always steelily polite in the way dyed-in-the-wool Tories are when dealing with Labour people. She was a governor of the church school but didn't really recognise that a Council estate had sprung up between her house and the church. Fielden, the eighteenth-century Halifax painter, and father of the more famous Copley, had painted Field House from across the valley for an earlier Stansfeld in the 1780s. His painting showed a space with a forest of trees between Field House and the church where so many plaques and gravestones commemorate earlier Stansfelds. It always seemed to me from talking to the last surviving Stansfeld that in her head nothing had changed: the Council estate which had replaced the trees just didn't exist.

She still maintained the tradition of garden parties for the community and the Tory Party. Indeed Maurice Macmillan, former MP for Halifax, once told me that these were one of the best parts of his tenure. But the last one was in 1972. I wouldn't like to think that my kids, Jonathan and Hannah, had killed this tradition, but they did misbehave atrociously, chasing round, getting in the way of the tennis and spilling food in the hall, all activities greeted with cool hostility, and "don't bring them again" expressions. It may only be coincidence that the party the twins wrecked was the last ever. Mrs Stansfeld never received visitors or gave parties again and died alone in 1987 aged 96, just after the heir to the hall and the last surviving male Stansfeld had died in Scotland the year before. So Field House, the surrounding buildings and the last remaining parts of the estate were sold off for less than £200,000 to Sir Ernest Hall who converted the servants' houses into bijou residences (price £180,000) for incoming executives and advertised them as "gracious living restored". At Haugh End the last Rawson, married, she said, to the "wild bull of the Pampas", is still alive, but everywhere outsiders moved in, not to the extent of the gentrification of Hebden Bridge, though for a long time the hills were alive with the sound of hammers as the old halls and farm houses were restored and improved for commuter families who moved into the best housing in the most beautiful part of the country, but spend most of their lives away from it.

This was hard times Sowerby and much of Jean's book is the tale of how its people adapted, adjusted and defied decline in a hundred ways. Some went onto the national stage, some emigrated, some developed new businesses and new jobs, some were content to grow old in their beautiful village with their memories. Which leaves Sowerby facing a new century physically unchanged but no longer quite the close little community it had been. Now it has become a peripheral suburb of Sowerby Bridge, itself a forgotten quarter of larger Calderdale. The dominant local families have gone, the new elite of commuters have no real involvement or roots in the community and, judging by the regularity of house sales, many don't stay in Paradise for long. The schools have grown and improved enormously but community facilities have declined. There are still cricket, tennis and bowling clubs but not much provision for young people except the out-of-school activities and facilities at the Ryburn Valley High and a youth club at Beechwood. The High School also puts on films for the over-50s but there are few pensioner facilities (moved to the Jagger Centre in Halifax), no social centre, no Post Office (moved down to Beechwood), two pubs fighting the decline of the pub trade, and six struggling shops. Here's a community with a website but without a centre, no hang out or meeting place and no focus to build community spirit.

Sowerby's people have endured the great de-industrialisation and demoralisation of the last three decades, some of the vigour and many of the characters described by Jean survive, but the young get educated and move away, those who remain find jobs in Halifax or live on benefits, and the old stay and become proportionately more numerous because they've nowhere else to go. All find life tougher and face further to travel to shop, or get to work and fewer jobs. The Council houses, now privatised to Pennine Housing, are better maintained and renovated but more of their residents are on welfare, a dependency culture, though I can think of far worse places to be dependent in than this, the most beautiful part of the most beautiful county, Yorkshire.

This is the chronicle of a Yorkshire village. I'm a Yorkshireman. I speak its language and know its quirks and what makes Tykes tick. I can't, however, claim to be a Sowerby native. I haven't lived there for the full forty years necessary to qualify yet, so I'm still an incumden and certainly no replacement for the squirearchy which has taken its hook and its money. My kids went to school in Sowerby, first to the Church School (now closed), then to Newlands (now flourishing as The Village School) and my lad was upset when we moved to Grimsby and he asked at school "When's us dinner?" No-one understood. I was delighted that my father's prayer book which I found the other day records the fact that he was confirmed on 6 March 1922 at St. Peter's, Sowerby. Indeed, he used to tell me how he was regularly sent up from school in the valley to take messages to Major Stansfeld. My mother's father, Austin Butterworth, a beer and spirits merchant at King Cross, used to supply Sowerby's then more numerous pubs before and after the First World War. I can claim some connection, though not full native status. I'll just have to admire the natives by reading Jean's chronicles of the independent-minded, tough, adaptable, and hard-working people of Sowerby over these years. It's fascinating. I advised her not to call her first book "Growing Up in Sowerby – And More". Being Jean and Yorkshire she did it anyway. But on reading this successor book I now have to say "more, more, more". Well done, Jean. You've brought Sowerby alive.

Contents

Introduction — 1

Family Matters — 6
My Father — 6
My Mother — 11
David Smith, My Brother — 13

Charm, Contests and Candy, Sowerby New Road — 21
Louise Dobson — 21
Christina Milnes (Tina McKay) — 21
Diane Judge (Parker) — 29

Memories of People and Places: — 35
Peter Ward's Recollections — 35
Haigh's Buildings — 35
Willie Lang — 36
Old Green Chapel — 37
School Days — 38
Ben & Fred Ackroyd — 40
Frank Broadhead — 41

The Greenwoods' Experiences — 42
The Lodge — 42
Disease — 43

The Bowers — 46
The Star Inn — 48

Sowerby Buses: Conductors and Drivers — 51
Eric Bartholomew (Bart) — 51
Ernest Mitchell — 54
Les and Brian Crossley — 56

Raymond Spencer — 57
Leslie Stead and the farms — 57
School Days — 58
"The Village" — 60
Wartime — 60
Games and Handicrafts — 62

The Kerridge family   64
John Kerridge   64
Vera Kerridge (Shaw)   71
Margaret Kerridge   76
   - Guides & Brownies   78

Upper Field House Farm, Triangle   82
The Moore Family   84
Christine Capstick (Mark)   86

The King family at Pitts Farm   89
Arthur Henry James King   89
The Great Blizzard 1947   92
Trees   98
Ian King   104
Hilda McCormack: Memories – Pitts Farm   106

The Fox Family   109
Sam Fox   109
Gavin Fox   120
Jo Fox   123
Ralph Fox   138

Feedback   139
Small World   139
The Traveller's Rest   139

Appendix 1: The Last "Old Green" Newsletter   141
Appendix 2: Old Sowerby   145
- Old cottages   145
- Sowerby in old postcards   146
- St Peter's activities   148
- Church Stile pub   149
- Town Gate   152
- Sowerby New Road   153
- Friends and Neighbours   154
- Park outings   157
- Housing   158

Illustrations

Many thanks to the people who loaned or allowed me to copy their photographs:

Eric Bartholomew
Marie Bateman
Dorothy Booth (Moore)
Christine Capstick (Mark)
Jackie Collins (Austin)
Veronica Duffy (King)
Sam Fox
Christine Greenwood
Irene Hirst
Diane Judge (Parker)
John & Vera Kerridge
Margaret Kerridge
David Kershaw
Ian King
Michael Lynch
Hilda McCormack
John Madden
Christina Milnes (McKay)
Pauline Mitchell (Addy)
Peter Moore
Eleanor Mount
Christine Myers (Brooke)
Michael Myers
Adrian Paley
Hazel Parkin
Blanch Riley-Gledhill (Helliwell)
Lynn Silcock (Medlock)
David Smith
Raymond Spencer
Sowerby Bridge Library
Sowerby Bridge Urban District Council Tenants Handbook
The advertisements for Astin's (p. 44) & Siddal & Hilton (p. 13) are from the *S.B.U.D.C. Centenary booklet 1856-1956*. The advertisement for the Louise Ltd ad (p. 17) is from an undated S.B.U.D.C. book.

Thanks to Felicity Potter for her editing, and to Kate and Si Claughan for their work on the photographs.

My thanks to Austin Mitchell for writing the Foreword to *Sowerby Tales*.

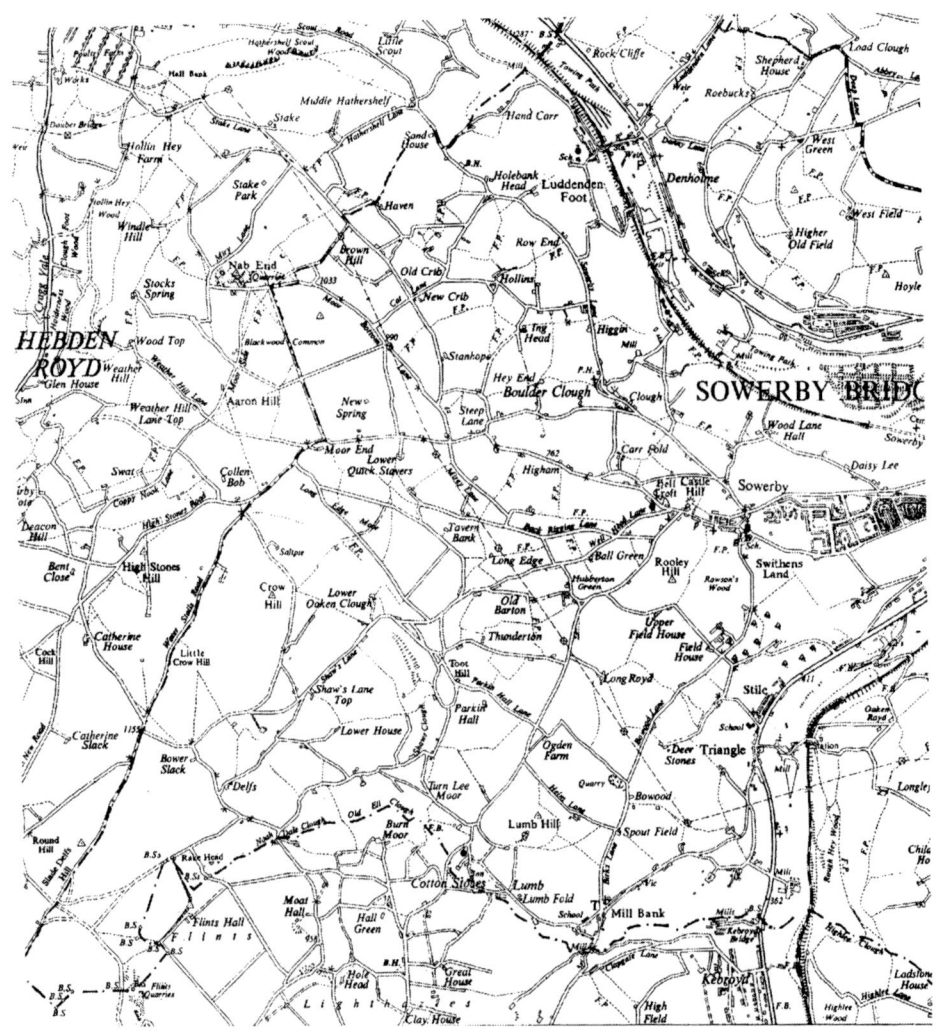

Map of the area from the Sowerby Bridge Official Guide 1956/7

Introduction

The response to my first "serious attempt" at writing and self-publishing my book *Growing up in Sowerby ... and More* has been both surprising and satisfying; the feedback has come from many sources and over distances! People have been kind with their comments and also helpful with answers to some of my queries. My writing has stimulated other people to reminisce and to write down their own personal memories and life experiences.

When I retired at the age of sixty on 28 May 2004 I had already decided that I would like to attempt to do some more "in depth" writing than I had attempted before. This would involve having to use a computer: I had handwritten a booklet previously about my senior school days, my next work would have more input and require some basic knowledge of using a computer.

Attending Sowerby Bridge Library on a "Learn Direct" course set me off on the right track. Years ago when our son James was a toddler I had done a little typing at classes held at Calder College, so I had knowledge of the keyboard. The rest of the set-up was a mystery. Progress came with the aid of our helpful library staff and realising that other people, no matter what age, were encouraged to master what they wanted to learn. Some people just wanted the basics to be able to e-mail family and friends; it was great to see people in their eighties achieving these skills, proving it is never too late! As the course became more in depth I found it difficult to have the "staying power" and did feel like packing it all in. The course had become rather "technical" for me and all I wanted to do was just get on and write!

Heather Karpiki the Chief Librarian came to my rescue and suggested that I take down all my newspaper cuttings of my letters to *The Evening Courier* and sit quietly and type them up and copy them onto a disc! I really enjoyed doing that, and felt as if I was moving on and getting somewhere.

The next step was to sort out a computer and where in the house it was going to be sited. Having used the model at the library, I thought one like that would fit the bill; also as I don't enjoy shopping very much, traipsing around looking at computers would come high on the list as being one of my worst nightmares! The easiest way to obtain one, or so I thought, was via the telephone and deal with the well-known company that way. Little did I realise that my call would go straight to an Indian call centre and I was speaking to a young man using an English Christian name who had a very pronounced Indian accent! He was most helpful and when I could understand what he was trying to explain – what I would need on my computer, i.e. Word, to do my writing on – we appeared to make some progress. Although I did worry a little after our conversation what I was going to finally end up with!

Some reorganisation of our dining kitchen furniture was necessary to accommodate the machine in a recess and create a small workstation. In due course a desk was purchased, the computer delivered and installed. So many wires to sort out, quite a taxing challenge for husband and wife to work together on without a "fall out" Next job was to learn how to use it on my own without any back-up or help. Why did I feel so apprehensive?

There followed occasions when I would shriek, "Oh no, it's all disappeared," the air becoming slightly blue! Nothing more frustrating than bashing away filling up that challenging blank page with words to see the screen empty again because you have pressed the wrong button! I soon learnt the importance of using "Save" and "Save as". Phone calls to James our son were frequent, as I would explain what I wanted to do and for some reason was unable to! He would tell me to try this, that or the other and eventually pennies do drop. Learning to use a computer is within everyone's capabilities; I really only wanted to use one to write and send e-mails. Use of the internet gradually was mastered as I gained more confidence. There are still many things I have no idea about on a computer but as long I can do what I want to do on it then I am happy! If you are pondering about learning to use one, join a course like I did, just keep having a try at doing things on it, you won't break it! Sending e-mail is an instant way of keeping in touch across the miles, although I do still love to receive a handwritten letter delivered by the postman, somewhat of a novelty these days, hopefully not a dying art!

There are many things that can distract a person from getting down to producing work at the keyboard: there certainly were in my case! The time of year can be an issue: if the sun is shining, then I want to be outside in the fresh air enjoying it. Autumn and the winter months lend themselves more to being sat in front of the screen working. The first year of my retirement proved to be productive; John my husband was still working. That meant with little interruption I could "crack on" with getting started on what I hoped would eventually turn into a book. In my mind I had already a title and knew exactly the picture I would like to use on the front cover. A list of the content subject material was drawn up; I had also another list of people to interview about their memories. My collection of photographic material was good, and included contributions other people had allowed me to have or copy for use.

* * * * * * * *

John retired during 2005: things were now different in the house! It did take some time for him to get used to the fact that when I am at the computer writing, I need to concentrate on that job alone. (Now I realised how annoying it must have been at times to the journalists in the newsroom at the *Evening Courier* when I worked there; I had to sometimes interrupt them whilst they were working at the keyboard.) It seemed at times that no sooner had I sat down to write than it was time for a coffee break, then lunchtime crept round and the evening meal had to be sorted! Working in the dining kitchen is not the ideal spot to be situated! Ladies from my generation are usually in charge of the meal making, doing the shopping and deciding what to buy, then preparing and cooking the food. Although I am capable of juggling several balls in the air at one time, Superwoman I am not. Slight alterations had to be made to enable me to get on with my work, needing at least four hours daily to produce something of substance at my computer. John has always helped with bringing in the shopping and doing the washing up: I am still working on the Jamie Oliver bit!

Life is full of little surprises; unfortunately the one that took place on 30th December 2006 was an unpleasant one! On Saturday morning, with no rush to get up, I gradually awoke to hear John announce as he paced the bedroom floor, "I have a pain, indigestion I think." Sleepily I asked if he had sucked a mint to see if that helped? He then announced that he thought he would drive himself onto Casualty at the hospital! Immediately I was awake and out of bed, and with a dreadful sinking feeling in the pit of my stomach, I threw on some clothes and joined him downstairs. He was now standing with the back door open to "cool down" as he was sweating profusely and had a grey pallor. As calmly as I could, although by now I had a pretty good idea what was taking place, I told him that an ambulance was necessary. This did not go down very well with my husband who said that I must not do that, but ring our son James at home in Southowram! In vain I tried to reason with him and to call 999 which again added to the very stressful situation – a position I never want to be in again! (What is it about men with ambulances? I don't understand the way they "tick" about being a patient in one.)

James was by now on his way to Sowerby, after a brief conversation when we all realised that John was having a heart attack. No further reference was made to calling an ambulance as it was making the tense situation even worse! Our son arrived and there followed a journey down Sowerby New Road through Sowerby Bridge, King Cross and down the side of the moor to the Calderdale Hospital Casualty department.

It was the most surreal journey I have ever endured, precious time when John was not having the medical attention that he was in need of; making me feel mentally wrecked, guilty and useless!

The medical staff quickly took over and John was admitted as a patient and over the next week tests were carried out that established that he would need a by-pass operation. What followed up to his operation taking place in Leeds on March 17th 2007 was a continual programme of help and support from the hospital which could not be faulted. Positive thinking and confidence in a wonderful surgeon saw us through a difficult time. My husband made a good recovery and we are extremely grateful to all the people who helped and guided us through this traumatic experience!

* * * * * * * *

Back to my book writing: I had now reached the stage where I was going to need some assistance with my chunk of about 30,000 words. This is where my friend Maggie Woods stepped in and "sorted out" my writing into a format and did some editing also. Maggie and I have been friends since working at the *Evening* Courier during the '80s and '90s. She was a feature writer and I worked in the media library at the newspaper. She returned the completed disc and at this stage I started to feel as if I really was going to produce a book! My next task was to find someone to print it for me – I didn't give a thought to finding a publisher. My booklet had been produced in Sowerby Bridge at Simprint, but when I approached Craig Simcock he said it was too big a project for him to take on. Knowing that my friend Trevor Simpson was having his book *Small Town Saturday Night* printed by a local firm, I contacted them and it was decided that they would take my work on. Unfortunately some time later a phone call from them made my spirits sink! The sheer volume and photographic content of Trevor's two editions was taking up all their time and my work could not be fitted in! I decided to go back to Sowerby Bridge Library and have a chat with Heather Karpicki who soon raised my hopes again. After a couple of phone calls she had a contact number for me of The Book Case in Hebden Bridge where I found the help I needed to produce my book. They took me on board during November 2007.

It was a joy to work with Felicity Potter, Kate Claughan and Peter Tillotson. Their help and expertise, relaxed manner and encouragement soon had the end product taking shape. Once the photographic material had been decided on, and then scanned in where it was going to be used and the covers sorted out, things were moving along. Discs and e-mails were exchanged until everything was as we wanted it to be. They also printed off a hard copy for me to go through: by this time one is having some mixed emotions, feeling excited and also a bit fed up of seeing and reading what you have written!

* * * * * * * *

To launch my book I decided to organise a "proper affair": although I had never been to a book launch, I have organised several events, usually school reunions or works Christmas parties. I soon ended up with about ninety names of friends and contacts to invite along to the Imperial Crown at Horton Street

Book Launch at the Imperial Crown Hotel, Halifax, June 24th 2008. Signing book copies with Mike Peel [Conner Photography]

in Halifax. After thinking through assorted venues for my launch, the Wallace Simpson Suite there was the ideal choice, and I knew it well as our son James and his wife Jane were married and had their reception and evening wedding party there on 30th October 2004

The launch was held on the 24th June 2008, with my friend Michael Peel acting as MC for the evening. The book signing and sales really made me feel as if I was now "up and running": the next day my books would be selling at The Book Case in Hebden Bridge and at Wade's Bookshop in Halifax. *The Evening Courier* had also published a feature by Virginia Mason about my writing the book. When you actually see your finished work on display in a shop window and on the shelves it is quite a thrill. Realising that I had also laid myself open to people's criticisms and comments is another "kettle of fish" to deal with!

My new book begins with some background to my upbringing and family life, and continues with a collection of Sowerby tales.

Mike, the MC for the evening
[Conner Photography]

Family Matters

My Father

My childhood years were mostly spent without the presence of my father. I have not many memories of him being around at our home 32, Town Gate, Sowerby where I was born; he left home when I was six and my brother David was 13 years old. Since publishing my book and speaking with an old friend of my father, I have learnt that it was he who delivered me in the early hours of 28th May 1944, at home in front of the fire. This had been a mystery to me and in all my lifetime my mother never told me who attended her when I came into the world a few weeks early all those years ago.

Dad – a passport photograph taken in 1951

It may seem strange that a couple who married on the 24th September 1935 at the Register Office in Halifax would part from each other during 1950 and not divorce until the 21st July 1972. They were "legally separated" for that period of 22 years: this seems incredible in today's times of quickie divorces and couples living together. I think deep down mother thought that there was no other man who could have taken his place. My father paid weekly to my mother to help with the upbringing of David and myself; if I remember correctly it was not a very substantial amount of money. My mother did go out to work to earn a wage, working part-time hours – she was usually home for teatime.

My father was born on the 20th January 1907 at Clay Clough Farm, Soyland. His parents were Isaac Smith and Ada formerly Hornby He was one of six children; his brothers were called Selwyn, Harry and Jack and his sisters Annie and Florrie.

The Smith family: L to R, Arthur, Jack, Selwyn and Harry. Seated, L to R, Florrie Cooke, Ada Smith and Annie Bradley.
Grandma Smith's 80th birthday party held at the Central Café, Hollins Mill Lane, Sowerby Bridge during 1954 – David and I were not invited!

He married my mother at the Registry Office in Halifax on the 24th September 1935 when he was 28 years old. His father Isaac's profession was a farmer and his mother's deceased father had been a paper-works labourer. My father had a friend called Trevor Dixon who also lived in Soyland; they had been out together one evening and Dad was given instructions by his father to be back home no later than 10 o'clock. He returned several minutes late to be greeted by his angry father who told him to go and spend the night with those he had been out during the evening with! Trevor took him to his home and Dad slept there sharing a bed with his friend, as that was the only space available.

On his return home the next morning he was then told to leave and go live with those he had spent the night with! Trevor's mother kindly took him in and fixed him up with some of Trevor's overalls and assorted clothing as my father had left his home minus any possessions. It was agreed that he would pay an amount for his keep and Mrs Dixon also helped him to buy some clothes. The family later moved to a detached house called "Spring Avon" in Ripponden Bank; he was lodging here when he married my mother, Emma.

On the 13th January 1919 my father was issued with a copy of his birth certificate for the purpose of the Factory and Workshop Act 1901. This was required for any purpose connected with the Employment in Labour or Elementary Education of a young person under the age of 16 years, or of a child; and this certificate was required for Employment in Labour. It was signed by Geoffrey Barker, a Schoolmaster at Norland Church of England School. My father was then aged 12 so this document was needed for any form of employment that he was about to do, perhaps working part-time in one of the many local mills that were active in the valley at that time. The fee charged to obtain the copy was 6d in old money.

My father worked for Beaumont's of Ripponden, where John Hirst was a boss. Later he became a coach driver at Ripponden and District. Trevor Dixon, his friend, married a girl called Matilda (Tilly) Crawshaw who lived a little higher up the road from him at The Cross, Barkisland where the road divides. She met my mother when she was courting my Dad.

Working as a coach driver for Ripponden & District Motors, mid-1930s. Dad in white coat on the left.

Tilly was surprised as she had known her from attending Barkisland Endowed Infants School, although not in the same class, my mother being a few years older than Tilly. She recalls my mother and another girl playing the piano at the school's assemblies. Selwyn Stott was the head teacher in the mid '20s. Tilly and Trevor were friends of my parents for many years; they married at Halifax Parish Church on 19th June 1940 and lived at Egerton Street before moving into a flat in Houghton Towers.

My father left my mother for another woman in 1950; she was called Louise Dobson and came from the Savile Park area of Halifax. She was born at 3, Raglan Street, Halifax and was the fourth child in the Dobson family. The eldest was Muriel, brother Nelson, then sister Marjorie, followed by Louise and younger brother Norman. Their father at one time was in charge of the Drill Hall in Halifax. Norman was born on the 5th May 1919 and later served in the Army for seven years in R.E.M.E (the Royal Electrical Mechanical Engineers) working as a signals engineer. Norman was a friend of my father's and eventually lived in a house he rented from my father opposite the garage Brook Foot Motors in Park Road, Elland.

I remember little of my father being at home even though I was six when he left. He had been the local butcher: the shop was attached to our house at 32, Town Gate. At one time he was in partnership, butchering with his brother Selwyn, as Smith Brothers, when Selwyn's family lived at Stones Farm, Dob Lane on the way to Steep Lane. (The shop was later sold to the Co-op for their butchery department; later this moved down into the main Co-op building, now Sowerby supermarket, Town Gate Stores. I only remember the Co-op owning the shop when Geoffrey Gledhill was the butcher there.)

My father had also run a taxi business and was known to "dabble" in various trades and was a bit of a "wheeler and dealer" also.

He began to socialise in the bar at the Palace Theatre where he met and became friendly with a variety of "upper middle-class" people. It was through these visits that he was introduced to Louise Dobson. This friendship developed into something more serious with the consequence of my father leaving my mother around the Christmas time of 1950.

It seems strange that this major event in my life holds nothing much to recall and I just became used to being a "one-parent" family. Deep down though I was always a little curious wondering what it would really be like to have a "dad" in the home!

During the '60s my father enjoyed the social scene and often visited The Ritz in Brighouse when it was a "Cabaret Club" and had visiting artists appearing.

Ritz Cabaret Club, Brighouse, mid-1960s
L-R: Dad, ?, Maureen Lidgard Brown, Bob Tiplady

Lyceum Nightclub, Bradford, mid-60s. L-R: Ann Hollingworth (a close friend of Dad's for many years) Dad, Maureen Lidgard-Brown (beauty queen from Lightcliffe, also a close friend), Bob Tiplady (Cycle shop owner Elland)

He was a member at several venues including, the Cabaret Club, 16 Oxford Street, Manchester in 1960. In Halifax he was a member of the San Remo Club, Back Victoria Street, Halifax and during 1964 he was a member at Sunny Vale Country Club, Hipperholme, Halifax. During September 1965 it was The Lyceum Cabaret Club, Bradford that he favoured (with a card also for a *Mrs Smith?*). Next an interesting card, a "Passport" membership at the Shanghai

Club & Restaurant, Marloes Road, Kensington, W8. The proprietors were Harvey Duncan Ltd. Here you were able to enjoy "Cocktails, Dinner Dancing & Late Suppers"! In August 1966 he joined the New La Ronde Club, 78-82, Halifax Old Road, Huddersfield. Here the Annual Subscription was for a Single – 2 guineas (£2-10p) or Double 3 guineas (£3-15p) The blue membership card described the venue as "Gayest Spot in Town" – this was of course before the word gay was "stolen" to describe something else! Finally he joined The Ebor Country Club, Huddersfield Road, Mirfield.

From conversations I have had with people who knew my father it seems that he had a big heart in helping others in their time of need.

A rare family group photograph, taken at a cousin's wedding in Rochdale, early 1960s. Dad, Mum, me and David

When John my husband and I married in December 1968, I never thought about inviting my father to attend our wedding. I felt that it would have been unnatural to have him "give me away" as I didn't really know him and it would have also put my mother into a difficult or uncomfortable situation. She had after all brought me up alone all those years, so my brother David gave me away in marriage. It was several years before I eventually met up with my father. Our son James was born in 1969; when he was about four years old we had called in at the garage Brook Foot Motors on Park Road to have a chat with David. During our visit he suggested that we call at the bungalow at the top of the yard where my father lived. So for the first time in many years I met him and introduced him to my husband and his grandson. He was pleased that we had "broken the ice" and was delighted to see us and visits to him continued up to his death in 1980. He was always pleased to see us and made us welcome.

My Mother

Emma Jane Smith was born at Booth Wood, Rishworth on January 16th 1913; her parents were Irvine Smith and Daisy née Willoughby. Her father had then been a "Journeyman" Paper Maker. (This title applied to someone serving an apprenticeship or not yet fully qualified.) The eldest child was Alec, then Albert and eldest daughter Ethel, followed by my mother Emma Jane, and Lucy was the youngest child. When Daisy was expecting Lucy, she left her husband with the children; he later died. Lucy was born on April 11th 1916 in Oat Street, Ingrow, Keighley.

Mother (R) with her sister Ethel, in the garden at the Council offices, Barkisland c.1921.

Mother at 32, Town Gate, Sowerby, c.1962

Daisy later married a man called Harry Butterfield; she went blind in 1945 at the age of 40. She lived in Keighley with Lucy and her husband Andrew and six children.

My mother and sister Ethel moved into the Council Offices in Barkisland, and because of the family problems she was brought up for some time by her Great-Uncle William Hepworth. They later moved to 1, Amisfield Road, Hipperholme, and she was married from here at 22 years of age. It was her Great-Uncle who taught my mother to appreciate good music and gave her confidence on a holiday to Llandudno to conduct a Brass Band playing in the Happy Valley Gardens one summer. Uncle later moved to Wyke where there was also a cousin of mother's called Olga. I remember going to visit there as a young child. What caused William to feature in mother's upbringing was never discussed or made clear to me.

*Barkisland Endowed Infants School, 1918.
Mother (with ringlet) aged 5 sitting next to girl with slate.*

Flowerland Pageant, Barkisland Church Group, 1925. Mother lying down at front, aged 13.

David Smith – My Brother

David was born on the 22nd June 1937; he attended Sowerby St Peter's Infant School and Bolton Brow Boys' Secondary School where he was a prefect and later School Captain.

When he left school in 1952 he worked at Dews Garage, Northgate, Halifax for two years. He then spent about the same time working at W.H. Smith, Union Street, Halifax, a wholesale newsagents. He then moved to work for Siddal & Hilton, Industrial Road, Sowerby Bridge, where hospital equipment was produced. The next working years were with my father at Brookfoot Motors, Park Road, Elland.

Aged about 9, c.1946. St Peter's School photo

When David was about 11-13 years of age and my father was still at home with us, he was involved with the feeding of cattle and horses which were kept on at Stones Farm, Dob Lane. My father had the farm on a tenancy from the Rawson family who at that time owned many of the farms and houses in the Sowerby area. When Dad and Mum had earlier moved to Sowerby from Soyland, his brother Selwyn and wife Violet with children Robert and Mary lived at the farm. That was when Selwyn and my father were in business together as "Smith Brothers Butchers".

Stones Farm: Above, Brian and Mary Exley, and me holding rein on "Ginger", c.1951. The spire of "Old Green" Chapel visible in the background.
Left, L-R: Kathleen Bohen, me, and Mary Exley.

Dad's sister Florrie helped in the shop along with my mother, and meat was also delivered to customers in the Beechwood Estate. David delivered the meat orders on Saturday mornings. When the Co-op later bought the shop, David had the job of showing the new man the delivery route.

My father kept about 10 cows for milking at the farm, also some horses.

An early start was made by Dad and David who left home around 5.30am to feed, water, muck out and attend to the animals kept there. The cows were milked by hand and the milk poured in churns to await collection from the dairy on Queen's Road. When David came home from school at teatime there would at times have been a telephone call from my father saying that he would not be returning home that evening. David had the job of going onto Stones to attend to the animals. This occurred throughout the year and often during the dark winter nights. Dad used to drop him off up Hubberton near the Red Brink with Shep our sheepdog. David with the dog collected more cattle kept for beef around the Crow Hill area and walked them across to Salt Pie. Father would have driven towards Steep Lane past the Traveller's Rest to the almost derelict building where the cattle were kept.

It must have been humiliating for my mother to witness Dad, Louise and friends riding down through Sowerby on horseback on a Sunday afternoon ride. His horse was called "Black Prince" and Louise's was an ex-police horse called "Ginger". The animals were stabled up at Stones Farm, where cattle were also kept.

Dad and Louise riding "Black Prince" and "Ginger" on the front at Blackpool, c. 1951 approx. They stayed at the Clifton Hotel.

During the war when food rationing was in force my father would transport meat over the border into Lancashire and supply hotels at the coast with "Black Market" meat that he had raised and slaughtered. Mother once told me that piglets were kept in the cellar at "Green Cottage" at the bottom of Rooley Lane when they lived there, before moving to 32 Town Gate.

Uncle Selwyn and Auntie Violet lived at Stones Farm at one time. Mr & Mrs Creamer with their children, Ivor and Maureen, followed them. Dad's brother Jack and his wife Melinda and family were next and then Tom Exley and his wife and children, Agnes, Brian and Mary. Later Arthur and Joyce Bottomley lived at the farm.

Father also at one time had a taxi service run from home: he kept his large black cars under a shed in the backyard at home and also in the yard on the left of Town Gate, before turning up Rooley Lane. Leading up to my father leaving home, David spent a lot of time with him and had been behind the wheel of a flat-backed wagon driving up on the tops from a young age!

David & taxi outside 32, Town Gate, 1946/7. The car is a Wolsley 12 HP OHV engine 1939 Model, Reg. CAK 544

When father eventually left home my mother bought David a Raleigh cycle from Cyril Sands, Wharf Street, Sowerby Bridge (Deli-Belge): this was to "soften the blow" of father's leaving. The money to buy it came from David's own bank account!

When father eventually left home in December 1950 he went to live in a flat above Charles Frederick Strecker's Butchers in West End, Sowerby Bridge, which he had now taken over.

Dad had taken an interest in Park Trading Company also in West End, where sweets and confectionary were involved. They moved into a large hut at the bottom of Sowerby New Road where David remembers sitting at a table and packing mints into rolls and packaging Choc Pops (similar to a Snowball). Dad tried to do business with Woolworth's to supply sweets but was unable to meet their demands. The business didn't flourish and eventually folded. (Earlier Lumb's Lollipops had worked from the hut and later moved into their premises at Old Cawsey, Sowerby Bridge.)

In the same yard at the rear was Sutcliffe's Joiners & Undertakers: this is now Jack Crossley & Sons, Sheet Metal Works. Above on the main road there was a small wooden hut, a newsagent's shop called Helliwell's which stood there for many years before being demolished. They sold sweets and cigarettes and newspapers in the shop. My friend Jean Crossley (Brayshaw) used to deliver the *Evening Courier* for them and recalls other school friends doing a paper round to earn some pocket money.

Whilst still living at West End, Dad set up Smith & Dobson where Louise sold stylish ladies' clothing and children's party style dresses. I have memories of going down to the place a few times, usually on a Saturday morning. This was my only contact with my father. At one time I was given a pale pink taffeta dress decorated with piping and fastening with a sash. Very pretty although not practical, it hung in the wardrobe and came out to be worn only a couple of times. Sewing alterations for customers were carried out by a lady called Millie Hawksworth who lived in Tuel Lane. During 1952/3 my father installed fittings into the rear hut including a Rayburn stove that heated the interior and the water. Also a bathroom was installed. The large rear room was furnished to live in. As the business progressed Dad left the butcher's shop and moved into the wooden hut. Sutcliffe's Joiners in the yard above altered the shop front and installed the front door flanked by windows for the clothes to be displayed.

Louise Dobson and Millie Hawksworth, to rear of wooden hut with Bentley car. Sutcliffe's timber yard on left, 1950s.

Dad was now dealing in motors and used to stand a few cars for sale on the land opposite where the Jehovah's Witness church now stands. David spent time with Dad, having a common interest in motors, and when David passed his test about the age of 19 was now involved part-time with father dealing in cars.

The animals at Stones Farm had now been sold; he still kept a few beef cattle in a field below the Golf Club at Norland. This was situated at Upper Harper Royd Farm and was rented from Roy Tatt's wife. Roy had been the last person with Willie Crossley (another friend of my father's) to deliver coal for Smith Wood in Sowerby Bridge by horse and cart. David had the job of attending to the cattle.

Christine Myers (Brooke) wearing a dress from Smith & Dobson, 1957. The dress was peach-coloured stiffened nylon with an underskirt, a narrow velvet ribbon trim around and above the waist. The patterned flowers and leaves had a muted glitter effect. Christine recalls that the dress hung beautifully!

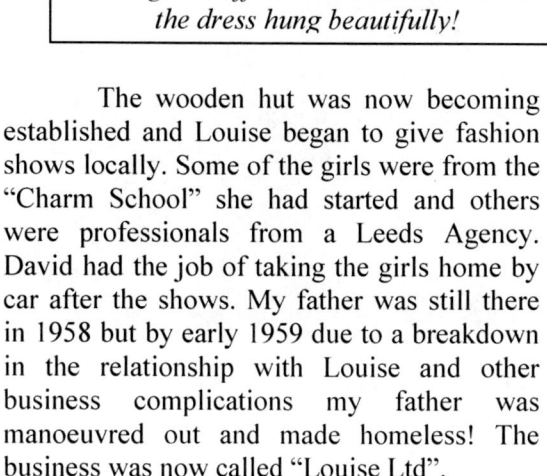

Pink taffeta dress from Smith & Dobson. Portrait taken by a photographer who came door knocking for trade in 1954. I was sitting on a piano stool in the front bedroom, with a sheet covering the large sash window.

The wooden hut was now becoming established and Louise began to give fashion shows locally. Some of the girls were from the "Charm School" she had started and others were professionals from a Leeds Agency. David had the job of taking the girls home by car after the shows. My father was still there in 1958 but by early 1959 due to a breakdown in the relationship with Louise and other business complications my father was manoeuvred out and made homeless! The business was now called "Louise Ltd".

Louise (SOWERBY BRIDGE) *Ltd*
SOWERBY NEW ROAD
SOWERBY BRIDGE
Telephone HALIFAX 81461

SUITS, COATS AND GOWNS
MODERN HAIRDRESSING SALON

Charm School for beauty and deportment

Party Time in the Wooden Hut, Sowerby New Road.

Louise Dobson at the head of the table raises a glass with friends at a party held in the rear room of Smith & Dobson, Sowerby New Road, Sowerby Bridge.

Dad and Louise at the head of the table with the party guests, during the 1950s.

Looking to Sowerby New Road and Sowerby Bridge from Quarry Hill, 1950s. The Wooden Hut (Smith and Dobson) and huts to the rear, also Helliwell's Newsagents hut with sunblinds – to the left, bottom of Sowerby New Road.

When times are hard an old friend can be the answer to the situation you are in: Mr McCarron the owner of Falcon Motors, Salterhebble came to his rescue and Dad was allowed to stay in an almost derelict cottage in the yard at his premises. Later he moved to live at The Grove Inn at Brookfoot (now Casa) where his friend Bernard Sales with his wife Gladys had the tenancy. Early in 1959 Dad moved into Grove Cottages opposite, he bought two of them on rental purchase. Around March 1960 David went into partnership with Dad and Bernard at Brookfoot Motors. In the early 1960's Dad converted a boathouse and a lock up garage on the premises at Brookfoot Motors into a bungalow, later moving in.

David lived at home until getting married on 28th July 1962 to his wife, also called Jean (Taylor) from Krumlin, Barkisland; they went to live in Elland. The wedding was one of the rare occasions when my parents were together at the same event: it was a little "awkward" as one can imagine. I had only seen my father on one or two occasions prior to David's marriage, one time at another family wedding of a cousin in Rochdale some years earlier and perhaps the odd sighting of my father in a pub somewhere up on the tops around Ripponden perhaps. There was no emotional feeling when I saw him; it was just like seeing any man I suppose!

L-R: Dad, Gladys Sales, ?, Bernard Sales, 1960s. Perhaps taken at a Licensed Victuallers' event.

Bernard retired from the business in 1969 to concentrate on his development of a motel at the Grove Inn having now bought the freehold. Father retired in 1972 having reached the retirement age. David continued with the business until his retirement in July 2000. The property was converted into Water's Edge Nursery in 2001.

Charm, Contests and Candy, Sowerby New Road

Louise Dobson

Louise married Leslie Morton who was then a transport manager for Kosset Carpets; They first met when he came to fit a carpet in the shop. The gown shop closed and the Charm School expanded and a school for models opened. She was then working from her home in Greetland. The business went on to be at the forefront in staging fashion shows and promotion events throughout Britain for designers, colleges and high street shops. Louise also worked within schools, teaching manners and deportment to young girls. Later, due to ill health, the agency was taken over by Bernadette Gledhill, a former model and a close friend of Louise's.

Louise died during January 2006, aged 88; the funeral service was held at Park Wood Crematorium on Tuesday the 17th of January and after at Bertie's Banqueting Room in Elland. The funeral was attended by hundreds of mourners. Louise had also worked hard for her favourite charity, the Church of England Children's Society.

* * * * * * * *

Christina Milnes (Tina McKay)

I visited Tina in her home 26/08/10 at Well Head Lane, Halifax.

Tina attended the same senior school as me at Sowerby New Road Girls' Secondary School; she was born in 1941 and lived in Russell Street, Sowerby Bridge. When she left school at 15 years old she began her working life in one of the many mills that were thriving in the valley in the '50s.

Her first job was at S. Dugdale, Holmes Road, Sowerby Bridge. They were cotton doublers. Here Tina worked as a "Doffer" – this was not a very pleasant job as it also involved thoroughly cleaning the looms when necessary. This was done with the use of water and having to lean across and into the workings of the loom to do the task thoroughly. Tina became caught one time and was injured, scraping and cutting under her arm and down her side. The accident unsettled her at doing the job, and she then decided to move on. She left and went to Wm. Edleston Ltd, Asquith Bottom; they were woollen manufactures, and also made items in cashmere. Her mother worked for Homfray and Co, carpet manufactures and was keen for Tina to work there and train to be a carpet designer. So her next move was to work at the factory on Walton Street as a pattern setter. Still accident-prone, she was unfortunate to trap her hand in a machine and sustain another injury!

In 1960 Tina's mum gave her a New Year's gift of a six-week course at the Charm School run by Louise Dobson at a cost of six guineas. Her mum was a customer at the wooden hut and bought outfits from Louise who allowed some customers to pay weekly instalments on their purchases; goods were held at the shop until the payment was completed. Ladies would call at the shop at the end of their working week to pay an amount off the clothing. I can vaguely remember being there one Saturday morning when Christine Brooke's mother Charlotte (Lottie) came into pay an instalment on an item she had "put away". From then on I was not allowed to be in the shop during a Saturday morning, Louise probably not wanting me to be aware of the H.P. arrangement she ran!

Tina enjoyed the company of about 10 other girls in the weekly classes, and told me the etiquette taught by Louise has stood her in good stead throughout her life and working career. Money was tight in their household and a further course of lessons could not be afforded, as things worked out Tina never had to pay anything else but continued at the wooden hut for some time.

Fashion Show at Forest Cottage, Cousin Lane, Ovenden 1950s. Swimwear from the shop. Louise Dobson sitting at the table, Tina Mckay 2nd from right

Around 1961 a hair salon opened to the side and rear of the shop. Advice on running a salon was given to Louise by Irvine Lodge, the well-known Halifax hairdresser, who was a friend of my fathers. Every day I wear a ring that used to belong to Irvine's first wife Vera: father bought the blue zircon stone ring set in platinum for my mother, and she later gave it to me when I was forty years old. Irvine and his first wife Vera's daughter Josephine features in my previous Sowerby book in a doorstep photograph when we were children. (Sadly Vera later took her own life.)

One of the Lodge's stylists called Peter Brattey came to work in the salon at the wooden hut for a time, later leaving to work on the P&O Cruise liners. The other stylist was a girl called Dorothy – she lived with her parents on a farm at Rishworth. A Sowerby girl called Biddy Gerhaghty served her apprenticeship and also worked at the salon. Tina by this time had started to assist Louise: she would shampoo customers' hair and manicure and paint their fingernails. As Tina was now "working", her future lessons were not charged for and she continued her classes free of charge. She became successful at selling clothing when she modelled items from the shop at shows, bringing trade and finance for Louise who by this time had "taken a shine" to Tina as she realised how good she was for business!

Fashion shows were held locally in Church and Chapel halls, schools and at Prince's Hall on Hollins Mill Lane.

Fashion show, Hebden Bridge. Rear: ?, ?, Hilda Parker, ?, Kathleen Bell. Front L-R: Louise Dobson, Tina Mckay, Ginny Wadsworth (Greenwood)

Tina left Homfray's to work at John Mackintosh's sweet manufactures in Halifax on November 13th 1961. She worked on a production line earning around £6 a week. Tina didn't care for the job and was not happy, and this resulted in her giving her notice – several times! The management refused to accept her requests to leave and eventually she was moved into a department to work alone on the Toff-O-Luxe production and here she now felt happy and more relaxed!

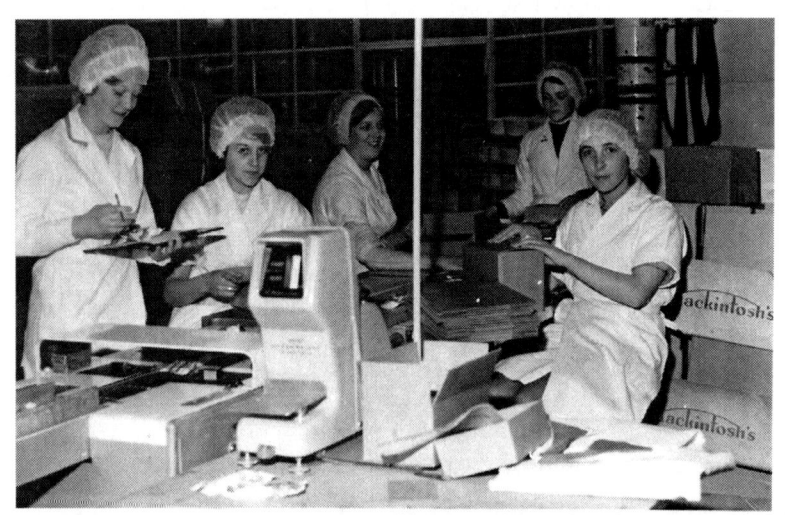

Tina (L) and friends working in G Mill at Mackintosh's factory in Halifax.

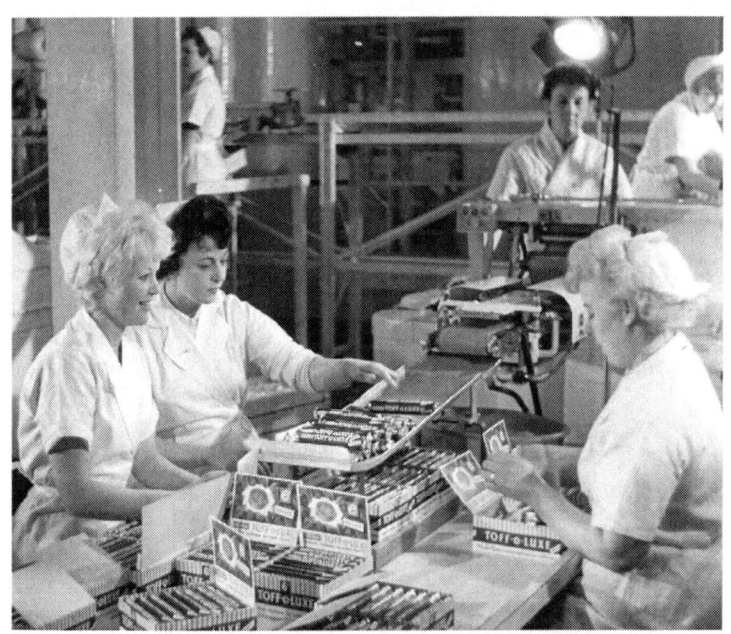

Filming for the Toff-O-Luxe Advertisement -- Tina on the left.

    It was in this department that a television commercial featuring Toff-O-Luxe (the toffees sold in a roll) was made. The film crew travelled to the Halifax factory to film the commercial and the sound was added later in London.

* * * * * * * *

On the 9th April 1962 Tina received an internal Departmental memo from Mr. J. Rothera. It read:

> Details for the visit to London are as follows:
>
> Train departs Halifax Station at 7.10am on Thursday, 12th April. Recordings will commence at 2 pm at A.B. Pathe Limited, Film House, Wardour Street, London, W 1.
> Accommodation has been reserved for you at the Bonnington Hotel, Southampton Row, London, W1. and we will return to Halifax on Friday afternoon, arriving in Halifax Friday evening.
> I will meet you at Halifax Town Station at 7am with tickets, seat reservation etc. (have copy)

During April 2011 I visited an exhibition held at Bankfield Museum to celebrate the 75th Anniversary of production of Quality Street in Halifax. A television was showing various adverts through the years for Mackintosh's sweet products; I sat down to view them. Sure enough the one that featured Tina came onto the screen, followed by another local girl called Angela Noonan who I recognised also.

Several weeks later on 29th May 2011 Tina and I visited the museum again so she could watch the advertisement for the very first time, all those years after it was made! It was lovely to sit next to her whilst she re-lived what had taken place in the factory during the filming of the ad!

She remembered most of the dialogue, we watched it through several times to check and hopefully it went as follows:

Yorkshire Film Archive & Nestle Heritage

Tina MacKay TV ad No 9 (Angela Noonan was No 8: Tina told me that several factory workers were filmed that day):

"I'm Tina MacKay; I'm a wrapper at Mackintosh's.
I help to keep the goodness in Mint Toff-o-Luxe.
The goodness like pure milk and butter and best sugar and the flavour of delicious mint.
We pack them into boxes of 14 pieces in a roll to keep in its goodness and flavour.
I'm a toffee maker so I should know. Try Mint Toff-o-Luxe yourself and really taste the goodness."

Tina's status at the factory went on to grow as she worked through all the aspects of quality control, becoming first a charge hand, then an assistant manageress, and finally a manageress. Tina worked at Mackintosh's for 33 years, leaving after many changes were enforced by the takeover of Mackintosh's by Nestle in 1994).

* * * * * * * *

Tina was still attending the Charm School and had now begun to enter "beauty" competitions. A report in the *Yorkshire Evening News* on the 24th August 1962 reported that 21-year-old Christine Mc Kay had been chosen from hundreds of pretty girls from all over Yorkshire to be entered in the Holiday Princess Contest, which was organised by the *Yorkshire Evening News* in conjunction with Butlin's Holiday Camp. The winner was to receive a free week's holiday at any of Butlin's Camps and also receive £10 spending money! Tina was now entitled to enter the weekly heat at a camp of her choice if she wished to, but decided not to enter further heats of the contest.

During 1962 the first Cortina car came off the production line and was introduced into Halifax by Smith's Garage, which was situated on Huddersfield Road in Halifax. Tina and another model from the Charm School were selected to be at the cocktail party held to celebrate the launch and "unveiling" of the new car. The models had dresses made in Oyster grosgrain satin with matching dyed satin shoes. The elbow-length gloves they wore were dyed turquoise to match the new Cortina!

The girls received gifts of boxed sets of five miniature French perfumes from the management.

Mackintosh's factories throughout the country ran a "Candy Ball Competition" Tina entered and won the heat, which was held at a venue in Menston. The prize was presented by Barney Colehan, of Leeds City Varieties fame. People from the theatre attended the event wearing their period costumes used when the show was presented. The girls entering the competition wore shorts and a blouse and were judged on their personality, appearance and deportment. All these things Tina had been taught by Louise at her classes. There were fourteen finalists who travelled to London for the event held at the Dorchester Hotel. Tina was placed third and a report and photograph taken at the wooden hut in Sowerby New Road for the *Daily Mirror* on 19th February 1963 reported that Tina was the first local girl ever to be placed in the first three of the competition.

Daily Mirror, 19th Feb 1963. Tina placed 3rd in the final of the National Candy Queen competition.

Candy Queen Competition. Local entrants, 1963. The winner Tina wearing sash, Ann Greenwood (placed 2nd) on her left, Angela Noonan sitting front right, Jean Lingard 3rd standing from the right.

Barney Coleham from the City Varieties Theatre, Leeds, gives a kiss to Tina, the new Central Yorkshire Candy Queen

The Halifax Charity Gala where Tina was dressed in the Mackintosh's period outfit was during the early 1960s. The costumes had been made previously; the man with her had appeared several times wearing his costume at other events.

Halifax Gala, 1960s. Tina and companion dressed in their "Quality Street" costumes with the Mackintosh float.

Diane Judge (Parker)

Taken from Diane's notes.

Diane, who now lives in Lytham St Anne's, was one of the girls who attended Louise's classes at her "Charm School" in Sowerby New Road. The course offered lessons in deportment and etiquette to young ladies at a charge of six guineas for six weeks' instruction. The classes were small, with only six pupils attending each session. Louise was glamour personified, she taught her pupils how to dress and to walk and sit elegantly. They were taught about table settings, menus and wines, dining out and at home, introductions, appointments, interviews, presentations and even how to meet the Queen! Louise explained to the girls that good manners were mainly based on consideration for others, and that they should treat everyone with courtesy. She treated all her students in exactly the same way, new pupils, mill girls or company directors' wives; she had time for everyone and gave each pupil her full attention. Her students got on well with each other; the classes were held in the large room to the rear of the gown showroom. Diane was also encouraged to expand on her creativity and dress the shop windows.

Pupils enjoyed the classes and signed up for further instruction, making more friends along the way. As the pupils gained confidence Louise had the "braver" ones among the girls modelling her stock of gowns at local charity fashion shows, these she produced and compèred with great style! The girls received no payment for doing the shows, but they were taken out by Louise and Leslie Morton, who by this time were married, to restaurants and to shows for treats which the girls enjoyed.

Fashion show in Hebden Bridge, L-R: Kathleen Bell, Diane Parker, Margaret Jackson? Hilda Parker, Tina McKay, Rita Parkinson?

Louise suggested that the girls wear a uniform of a dark blue blazer, white skirt and a straw boater hat: the models loved it and the team became quite a feature at local events. Diane remembers Christina (Tina) Mackay, Enid Furness and Annette, a bubbly redhead from Elland. When larger-sized more mature models were required, Diane persuaded her Mum to take part, along with other mums, Audrey, Millie and Kathleen Bell. Later Louise opened a popular hairdressing salon in another back room and Diane remembers Andrea Howley of John Street West, Sowerby Bridge working here. Hairstyling and make-up displays were added to the team's expanding repertoire. Diane observed and learnt about combing out hair, a skill that has remained with her all her life. There was no shortage of willing volunteers for having their hair styled.

Diane asked Louise her opinion about entering the Bradford heat of the "Miss England" contest; she encouraged her and also went along to the heat with Leslie to support her. She didn't win a prize but learnt from the experience and went on to win second place and a cash prize in the following week's Rochdale heat. One week later she won the qualifying first place and more cash at Burnley, and a month later was stunned to become runner-up to Miss England in the London final! As summer approached, Diane decided to give up her office job to work part-time at a garage, thus enabling her to enter the northern seaside national beauty contests. The girls she met were great fun to be with, and modelling work was often passed on. It was then that Diane decided to model professionally as she now had the training and the confidence to do it. Her feet were now firmly planted on the ladder of the "Beauty Circuit" and she went on to regularly win cash prizes and other items.

Early in her competition events she won the Bradford Lido Queen. This was held at the open-air pool in Lister Park; the prize was £50! Most towns at that time held some kind of contest; the one at Bradford was a little different being a swimsuit parade around the lido. Bradford and Sheffield also held "Press Balls"; each had a "Press Ball Princess" where dresses were worn. Diane won both of these contests. The prize was £50 each and £50 to spend on woollen clothing from a dress shop in Bradford. That amount enabled her to buy two suits and a coat; at Sheffield she also with her cash prize received a canteen of cutlery which served her well for years!

Her first national contest win was Southport's English Rose in 1964 plus £500 cash. Here the girls had to parade in dresses and swimsuits. It was also the first contest to give members of the audience a voting slip and participate in choosing the winner. Diane's win enabled her to buy a second-hand Ford Anglia; she was thrilled to become the first member of her family to "have some wheels". She also said "Goodbye" to her boyfriend and his motorbike!

Diane had become friendly on the beauty circuit with another local girl, Maureen Lidgard-Brown from Lightcliffe. Maureen was also a friend of my father's; he used to transport her to beauty competitions at various coastal resorts.

When the girls used to travel by train to the competitions together, the return fare to the coast was 13/6 (67.5p) in old money for a return ticket. The organisers usually provided a ham tea after these seaside competitions, which they always enjoyed! Venues were Bridlington, Blackpool, Fleetwood, St.

Miss Britain 1962 contest: Diane wins the heat at Burnley. Helen Shapiro promotes the hair spray!

Diane, winner of Miss Dunbar, Scotland 1966.

Anne's, New Brighton, Southport, Rhyl, Dunbar, Ayr, Margate and Morecambe. All these had weekly heats to enter, so for Diane living in Sowerby Bridge the access to most of the towns was good.

Other titles she won include Miss Halifax Bowl, Dairy Maid of Halifax, Tea Queen of Doncaster, Oldham Carnival Queen, Miss York, Miss Burnley, Miss Blackburn and Miss Bolton. These contests usually offered a £50 prize plus "goodies" for the girls. The larger national prizes with heats were more lucrative: "Miss Sunny Rhyl" in 1966 offered prize money of £250, a gold watch, an assortment of goodies, plus a full wardrobe to take part in the Miss International contest. This was held at the Mayfair Hotel in London for a week, and involved shopping for clothes etc.

Next they flew BOAC to the Bahamas for a week to the Sheraton Hotel. Whilst in the Bahamas for the competition Diane was contacted by the Smith family: Arthur worked at Nassau Airport Control, and he was originally from Sowerby Bridge. Diane knew his sister Gladys and her mum knew another sister called Connie; they lived on Albert Road in Tuel Lane. After the competition Diane enjoyed a few days of sight seeing with them.

The contest was won by a German girl, which was no surprise to Diane as Germany appeared to dominate the entrants and most of them prior to the competition had submitted glamour photographs of themselves. The previous winner had also been German; it appeared the whole contest was geared towards promoting the Bahamas Tourist industry to appeal to Germans at that time during the '60s as they were the ones who were venturing abroad and spending money.

Miss International competition, in the Bahamas.

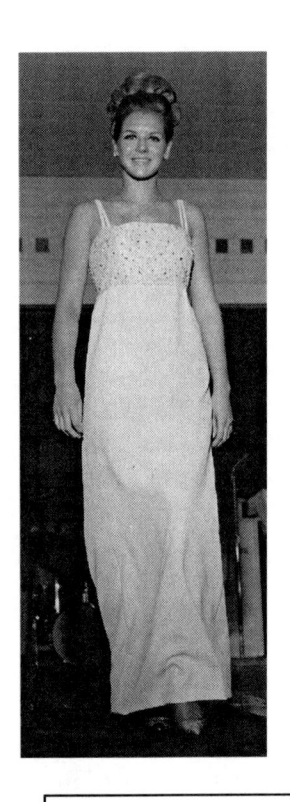

The Evening Wear section.

Looking lovely – posing in a wicker chair.

Representing her country, Number 8.

Diane's other wins were Miss Fiesta Club, £100; Miss Dunbar (Scotland) 1966, £100; Miss Rainbow Club of Bradford, £250; Cleethorpes Gala Queen £100; Miss Andre Phillipe 1967, £100 plus lots of goodies and a week in Amsterdam with tours, single rooms in a 5-star hotel for Diane and her boyfriend Pete (later husband); the Sunday Mirror Summer Beauty Queen, £250 (this was held somewhere down south); the Lucas Gala Queen 1968 – an annual star-studded event at held at Burnley, in which entrants were invited to take part, and had to already have a title. Diane's last national win was Miss Margate in 1968 winning a £250 cash prize. This was used to purchase a settee and chairs which after re-covering several times are still in use today!

Most of the beauty contest heats paid a cash prize of £25 for a win, £15 for second and £10 for third, enabling girls to make a tidy sum of cash from winning a prize and then returning to try again! At these heats were selections of prizes provided by the various sponsors for the winners. Diane was never short of hairsprays and shampoos, make-up and perfume, flowers, jewellery boxes, watches, chocolates, champagne, dozens of bottles of fruit juice, ice buckets, drinking glasses, vouchers for clothing, travel and vanity cases. Cigarettes were also offered as a prize: these were passed onto Diane's mum!

When Diane looks back on her beauty contest days, she recalls how much fun it all was: girls were not upset at losing out. It was usually the same girls who were entering the contests, some you won, and some you didn't! Most of them appeared to do well and win enough to keep them happy. The summer months were more lucrative with the Miss United Kingdom and Morecambe's Miss Great Britain offering prize money of £1,000 to be won. Miss England and Miss Britain (Mecca) were important sounding titles, but the prize money was only about £200, also girls were not allowed to compete in any other contest in this country for a year. Exceptions were Miss World and Miss United Kingdom, the exclusion from entering other contests denied the girls the opportunity of other wins when they were at their best, a case as Diane put it, of swings and roundabouts!

Her last national title, 1968 Margate

In 1964 as mentioned earlier, Diane won her first big national contest, and the prize money enabled her to stop working at the garage, buy a car and take on more photographic, TV, and wholesale fashion modelling work. Keeping busy with all these things Diane saw less of Louise, but managed to help out with teaching at the Charm School, now held at Louise's home in Greetland, whenever she could.

Diane married Peter Judge in April 1968: they met when she worked as a petrol pump attendant at Cromwell Garage, Brookfoot. They have daughters Samantha, born October 1970, and Suzanne who was born in October 1972. Losing touch with the modelling world, she enjoyed being a mum! In 1973 she qualified as a dance and exercise teacher, a job she loved which also fitted in well with family life. She continued doing this very successfully until retiring in 2002. Throughout her teaching career she used Louise's all-inclusive teaching style, and just like her, always turned up on time, looking her very best, preparing her lessons thoroughly and giving her students 100% of her attention. Diane likes to think that her classes were as popular as the ones that she attended at the wooden hut at the bottom of Sowerby New Road, where the seeds for her success in life were sown!

Memories of People and Places

Peter Ward e-mailed me during October 2008 from his home in Scarborough. He was recovering from an operation on his shoulder, and after reading my book he sent me some notes based on his own memories. Peter's elder brother Mike (Stuart) Ward now runs The Actors' Workshop in Halifax with his wife Lottie.

Peter Ward

Haigh's Buildings: Demolished during the '50s

Two men were responsible for "taking the building to pieces" – they were called Ralph and Steve. Whilst working on the project they stayed at The Shepherd's Rest pub at Hubberton where Peter's father George Ward was the landlord from 1954 for over 20 years helped by his wife Lillian. The men stayed at the pub for quite a long time; every three weeks they would have a weekend visit home to County Durham to see their families.

The Shepherd's Rest at Hubberton was also known as "The Riggin": the word has nothing to do with ships. A gentleman informed me that it meant "shoulder" as in "situated on the shoulder of a hill". The word derives from the Old English word Rigge or Hrycg, both meaning ridge. The origins of the word began with the Anglo-Saxon tribes in Britain, when people lived near to a ridge. It is also a surname.

Mr and Mrs Ward became friendly with the men and their wives, who would occasionally come to visit Sowerby for a weekend stay. Peter does not know where they all stayed on these visits; perhaps somewhere in the village.

> **Haigh's Buildings**: situated in Town Gate, originally one building and later made into dwellings, no.s 47 -51. During the demolition to prepare for the building of the Council Estates it was discovered that within the 17th-century stonework was the timber frame of a 14th-century hall. It was dismantled and the beams numbered to be rebuilt at Barnard Castle Folk Museum (later Beamish Museum). Sadly this was never carried out and this piece of Sowerby history was lost for ever.

Willie Lang

When George Ward reached five years of age, both his parents had died. His father's sister Annie Ward had married Jim Hardy and they brought George up.

Another cousin brought up by them was called Willie Lang He later lived at Haigh's Buildings and became an acclaimed musician. Peter has fond memories of the gentleman, and he stayed at his home once in Stockport, Cheshire, when he was playing first trumpet for the Hallé Orchestra. Peter at one time was taken along to an old warehouse in Manchester where they used to rehearse. As they climbed up the staircase to the practice room they met a strange-looking man who was muffled up in a large coat and scarf and wearing a large hat on his head. Peter was then introduced to Sir John Barbirolli! Sitting at the rear of the room Peter listened to the orchestra playing "Austria"; John Barbirolli suddenly stopped them playing and selected one musician to tell him he was playing, "da,da,da,de,da" instead of "da,de,da,da,da". Peter was amazed that he was able to pick out one man from the orchestra when they were all playing together! Willie Lang used to relate many funny stories about his touring days to Peter.

When Peter was learning to play the piano he dreaded Willie calling in at the house if he was practising at the time. He would criticise him, especially so if he was learning to play The Trumpet Voluntary. Willy Lang never had a music lesson in his life and went on to be champion cornet player of Great Britain three years running when he played with the Black Dyke Mills Band. Besides playing with the Hallé Orchestra he also played with André Previn and the London Symphony Orchestra. Peter had lost track of him but then found out that he was living in Harrogate. Peter contacted him and he and his wife Joan were privileged to visit him on a number of occasions. He has also had contact with Willie's second wife Anne and their four sons, Michael and Patrick from his first marriage, to Muriel, and Gerald and James from his second marriage.

William Lang, known as Willie Lang, lived in the top house (facing into the fields at the rear) at 47 Haigh's Buildings when I was a little girl. He was born at Hollin Well at Norland in 1919. He came to Sowerby when his father died when he was eleven years old and lived in Beechwood with his Aunt Annie Hardy. His mother Esther Ward was her sister and a sister of George Ward's (landlord of The Riggin) father. They came to stay for Easter and ended up staying for two years!

The first "instrument" he tried to play was the rubber hosepipe from his mother's wash tub! Later when he had a proper instrument he played in Norland Band and also Bradford Band from an early age, and when he was sixteen became the assistant principal cornet player at Black Dyke Band, Queensbury, the renowned brass band of John Foster's Mill, Queensbury.

He was employed as an apprentice stonemason at Parkers in Sowerby Bridge and excelled at his work, earning a tradesman's wage while he was still a boy. He worked on the stone columns of the former Barclay's Bank in Sowerby Bridge. Joining the Royal Engineers in 1941 he served in Austria, Italy and North Africa for five years. He was a tank commander for the 1st Field Squadron Royal Engineers in the 8th Army. When he was demobbed in 1946 he returned to the Black Dyke Band and became a champion for his role as principal cornet player from 1938-1941, 1945-1950, and 1952-1954. During this time they won the National Championships of Great Britain in 1947, 1948 and 1949. Willie Lang was also the All England Solo Champion in 1947, 1948 and 1949. During 1950 he left to play with The West Riding Orchestra until returning in 1952.

Later he joined the BBC Northern Symphony Orchestra; in 1953 he joined The Hallé Orchestra as third trumpet. He then went on to be principal trumpet player with the London Symphony Orchestra. He also worked in the film and music industry with well-known people including The Beatles; during 1968 he played on their number one record, "Hey Jude". He also worked with musician Frank Zappa and Mike Batt of The Wombles fame and also John Williams on the sound track of *Star Wars* in 1977 and the Superman films. He worked on William Walton's music for *The Battle of Britain* and other films including *The Guns of Navarone* and *Where Eagles Dare.*

Geoff Whiteley, administrator at The Black Dyke Band, said that he would be remembered as a top-class musician, either the greatest or one of the greatest musicians of all time.

In a distant memory I recall a post horn hanging on a red cord on the wall of the cottage where they lived in Haigh's Building. His triple tonguing was exceptional. "The Post Horn Gallop" was his "pièce de resistance". The Medlock family next door were entertained on many occasions when he was rehearsing his music, the sound carrying through the dividing wall of the house! As young children we would sit on the wall in front of his house and listen to him play.

Old Green Chapel

Peter attended Old Green Chapel from quite a young age; this was when the family lived at 6, Thorpe Place, Hubberton. This row of twelve cottages had been home at one time to weavers who worked by candlelight at their looms. At the end house, No. 5, lived Mr and Mrs Heap with their children Mary, Michael and Gwyneth. It was Gwyneth who took Peter along to the chapel; she used to look after him quite a lot as a small child for Mrs Ward.

Peter does not remember when he stopped attending Old Green. His great friends the Laycock brothers were regular attenders there (Trevor, Brian and Geoffrey). Peter's parents never attended church when George lived with Grandma Hardy (he always called her Mother, never Auntie).

He was brought up as a Catholic. Lillian his wife had attended Zion Congregational Church at Ripponden: when the couple married, the families "fell out" due to the differing religions. As a result neither attended a church again. Peter was allowed to attend various places of worship to "find his own place", settling eventually at Steep Lane Baptist where he was baptised at the age of 21 in 1963. Since moving to Scarborough he now attends the United Reformed Church there: this is the former Congregational Church so the full circle has been completed!

School Days

Mrs Albrighton was Peter's first teacher at St Peter's Infants School, Sowerby. She was also his favourite teacher over the years; he thought she was a very kind lady. Peter was given the job of ringing the school handbell on his first day, for the children to line up and go back into school after the dinnertime break. Unfortunately he managed to hit a few on the head with it before it was taken from him! He also had a "dagger" which he had made and took along to school the next day. The children who escaped being hit on the head with the bell were "stabbed" with the "dagger"

Mrs Ward soon had an appointment to see the headteacher Mr Wright about her son's behaviour. Peter liked the head teacher and says he soon forgave him for his naughty ways! He also got on very well with Miss Connie Taylor, one of the teachers. [See her obituary overleaf.] Peter was very clever at arithmetic and knew his tables inside out – these were chanted out at home until perfected. He remembers racing to complete his sums as the reward was being allowed to take the foil tops off the milk bottles! The winners were usually Peter and John Madden.

The teacher to dread was Mr Ingham: pieces of chalk, the board rubber, even the odd chair would be thrown by this man when he was angry or wanted attention. It was a strange way to teach children; even so Peter and other pupils would walk down Pinfold Lane to meet him in the morning and walk up to the school with him.

Mr Proctor also rated high on Peter's list; he was without doubt a patient, lovely man who managed to bring out the best in his pupils. In our final year at Newlands School there were, according to Peter, ten pupils who passed the eleven-plus examination to attend Sowerby Bridge Grammar School, the best number ever from Sowerby.

The dinner ladies are well remembered, especially Mrs Smith from Stocks Lane – she distributed cuddles when they were needed (not allowed today) – Mrs Paley, Mrs Tetley and Mrs Easton; also Mrs Cardwell who insisted Peter ate up his cabbage, which made him sick! Years later when Peter worked for the Prudential and collected from her house on Pollit Avenue, he related his trauma about the cabbage, but Mrs Cardwell was not for moving on the subject and said "it would do him good". Strange, how as a child these memories of having to devour ghastly things stays in your mind a lifetime.

Taken from her obituary in the Halifax Evening Courier:

*Miss Constance Mabel (Connie) Taylor celebrated her 100 birthday during January 2009. She died at Ingwood Nursing Home, West Vale on 23rd March 2009. Her funeral and burial were held at St Bartholomew's Church on April 24th 2009; she had previously lived in Ripponden. During her career she had taught at several schools in the area, including Ripponden Junior and Infant School, and Norland Junior and Infant School. She became the head of New Road Primary School and Tuel Lane Infants School, Sowerby Bridge. She dedicated her life to the education of children, and inspired generations with her teaching. She sang in the choir at St Bartholomew's Church in Ripponden for eighty years, which is a remarkable achievement; she was also a member of the church council. She also sang with the Elland Hospice Choir, was a founding member of the Rishworth's Women's Institute, a member of the retired Teacher's Association and Halifax Antiquarian Society.

Ben & Fred Ackroyd

Ben and his brother Fred were two of Peter's favourite people: they used to be regulars at The Riggin Pub at New Barton, Hubberton, when his parents George and Lillian were the licensees (from 1954 – over 20 years). He remembers happy hours playing dominoes with them in the taproom. When they lived at home with their mother and father, Fred would attend to all the housework. Peter used to call at their house on his way home from school. Peering through the window to see if Mrs Ackroyd was in the room, he would tap on it and she would shout him to come in.

Fred was then instructed to find Peter some sweets! He thought her a lovely lady but rather reminded him of someone who was "looking for a fight" as she was always pushing her sleeves up!

Fred's annual treat was on Christmas day at lunchtime in The Riggin when he lit up a big cigar. This was the only time during the year that he had a smoke. Peter had as much pleasure watching him puff it as Fred did smoking it!

Ben died aged 95 on the 9th of January 2010, peacefully in his sleep at Alexander House, Savile Park, Halifax where he had been a resident for several years. His funeral service was held at St Peter's Church, Sowerby on 18th January followed by cremation at Park Wood, Elland. Mary his sister, aged 90, gave a tribute to Ben: it was poignant and humorous. She related how Fred was the more generous of the two brothers. He would give a small child a sixpenny piece, Ben would then give the child a threepenny bit, only to retrieve it saying, "Here, take this one, it is bigger", handing the child a penny!

The Ackroyd brothers came from a large family of 10 children, they lived at 6, Rooley Lane, Sowerby. Later Ben and Fred moved into a cottage together during 1978 in Wesley Place situated in the yard at Rooley Lane Chapel. They remained bachelors all their lives, although Ben did once propose marriage to my mother! It was Fred who did the daily chores of cooking, baking, cleaning and washing. Ben had a farming background and also worked as a wagon driver for many years travelling all over the country. Fred worked at Sagar Richards down in the valley; as he walked to work he whistled happily! They both spoke with strong broad Yorkshire accents and were certainly a couple of the "characters" in Sowerby. Their favourite social place was the taproom of the Shepherd's Rest, known as The Riggin at Hubberton (now converted into cottages).

Frank Broadhead

Another local character at The Riggin was Frank Broadhead. He was born in 1900 and died in 1968; he was Muriel Maskill's father. He came from a large family of 11 children of which only 8 survived.

Like his father before him he was a talented musician, he also sang in cinemas to accompany the silent movies. His employment was varied, horse and cart haulier, butcher and at one time he worked at Collinson's tea warehouse in St John's Place, Halifax. He had a fish shop in Haugh Shaw Road, where he also trained other fish fryers.

Frank was quite a comic and often had the company at The Riggin in uproar. Something would crop up in the general conversation that was going on and Frank would say, "Now this is true": the place fell silent, dominoes were put down onto the table Frank would relate an outrageously funny tale. One of them was as follows, the West Indians were playing cricket in England. At the time they had the three W's playing for them, Worrall, Walcott and Weekes. England had been given quite a thrashing, hitting the ball around the boundary, scoring fours and sixes. Drinkers were discussing this when Frank piped up, "Now this is true, I have the longest knock in cricket. I once hit the ball and it landed in a tram at King Cross. They chased the tram around Halifax for a week whilst me and my partner ran a thousand runs. We were playing up Pellon at the time." Customers were rocking with laughter but Frank hadn't finished yet! He went on to relate a story about going to the races with his brother; they left the house telling their mother that they would be home for tea. They arrived home twelve months later, having visited every racecourse in the country, winning a million pounds, and then losing it all! Peter was once sent to Frank's home on an errand by his mother. Their corgi dog followed him up the street and into his house. Frank's false teeth were on the hearth, where he used to put them – the corgi found them and promptly chewed them up!

* * * * * * * *

I was saddened to learn of Peter's death on Christmas Day 2010 aged 66. He was awaiting further heart surgery in the New Year. Peter and his family had lived in Scarborough since 1985; he used to return to Sowerby and visit the places he loved. Walking to Crow Hill, attending the Anniversary service at Steep Lane and meeting up with former school friends brought him great pleasure.

The Greenwoods' Experiences
As related by Christine Greenwood

Christine Greenwood was the youngest child of Rachel Annie née Johnson and Harry Greenwood. They lived at 42 Triangle Row next to the local Co-op on the main road. It was a very basic home with no comforts; the toilet block for the row was at the back of the Co-op. There was no back door so Christine would get out of the back bedroom window to play on the grass at the rear. There was a bare stone staircase leading to the upper floor, and rats would run up and down it! Mrs Greenwood became an expert at catching them and would hold them down with her foot on their neck, then kill them with a blow from a brick! The bodies were then taken by Mr Greenwood to be burnt on the furnace at Morris's Mill, Triangle.

It was here that Mrs Greenwood had come to find work from Askern, South Yorkshire as a thirteen-year-old girl during the early 1920s. Mrs Austin who lived opposite across the island at 33 The Newlands also came from the same village. The village was a mining one and the work situation was poor. Mrs Greenwood was an early riser and used to wake the girls up in the morning to start the day's work on time. The habit of rising early continued through her life and Christine recalls setting off for work in later life at 7am and taking freshly-baked scones and buns for the girls at work, the washing already blowing on the line! Her mum had boundless energy and drive, I remember her also being a very kind and caring person who had always an interesting story to relate.

Mr Greenwood worked on nights for twenty years as an overlooker at Morris's in the very noisy environment of the weaving shed at the cotton mill. He had worked there from twelve years old as a part-timer, attending school in the mornings, then working in the mill during the afternoons. He had not been called up to do any National Service, as he was blind in one eye, the result of a childhood mishap with another boy. Many girls came down from Scotland, Durham and Doncaster to work at Morris's and lived at the Hostel there.

The Lodge
This was earlier the mill owners' house called The Lodge and dated from the early 1800s. In 1851 William Morris (44), his wife Barbara (30) with their two young children, and three servants were recorded on the census. It opened as a residential hostel in 1921 and had 24 bedrooms with facilities to cater for over 100 people. The large detached house below Triangle School was also used as an "overflow" to accommodate some of the young women. Many of the hostel girls courted local young men and went onto marry and settle in the area. During the 1980s The Lodge was converted into apartments and renamed Stansfield Grange.

Disease

Living in such poor housing conditions at Triangle Row, the health of the occupants was at risk and children were most vulnerable to pick up diseases. Fred was the eldest child: he was born in 1934. He had Scarlet Fever as a young boy and was sent to an Isolation Hospital in Todmorden. At twelve years of age he went to stay on a farm in Buxton to be "built up"; here he was fed good food, tasting butter for the first time in his life.

Joan, Christine's elder sister, was born on the 12th February 1932. At the age of nineteen in 1951 she contracted Tuberculosis. Her mother thought that the source of the disease was from the milk delivered by a local farmer: this was before the introduction of T.T. tested milk. Other local children also became ill with the disease. The milk was simply ladled out of the churn into a jug which the customer had left out on the doorstep or window bottom for that purpose. It would perhaps be covered by a linen cloth to keep out any flies or dust. The treatment for Joan was to have one of her lungs collapsed for three years, and have bedrest, good food and plenty of fresh air. She had a bed downstairs while she recuperated from her illness, sheets were changed daily: no fancy washing machines then, just the sheer hard work of the old fashioned method of washing with mangle and dolly tubs.

Her illness secured the family's move to Sowerby, into a modern Tarren House at 26 The Newlands: a house previously lived in by my lifelong friend Beryl Waddington.

Beryl's mother Ena died in 1951 and later around 1952/53 with her Father Rennard and brother Robert moved to 22 Norland View in Bolton Brow. The move was to enable Beryl and Robert to be looked after before and after school by relatives who lived in East Parade. Mr Waddington worked at Blackburn & Sutcliffe in Kebroyd.

When Christine was a baby of seven or eight months, she was lying in her pram and a visiting relative became concerned at her appearance. She was listless and had little interest in anything, so Mrs Greenwood decided to take her onto the Hospital to be checked over. The only thing they could find was a tiny spot on the back of her neck. Mrs Greenwood was about to leave the Hospital when she was summoned back by a nurse and asked if she was breastfeeding her baby? She replied that she was, and was then requested to leave Christine in the hospital. Next day when she went to feed her baby, Christine was now covered in sores and spots on her legs and armpits. Mrs Greenwood continued to visit daily to feed Christine, until she recovered. Never sure of what she had been poorly with at that time, Christine thinks it was perhaps a form of blood poisoning, septicaemia or meningitis that struck her down.

Christine left Ryburn Secondary School in 1959 and went to work as a flat machinist at Astin's on Burnley Road (now Spencer's Trousers, Friendly Works, Sowerby Bridge). Her working hours were 7.45 am-5pm Monday to Friday and her first pay was £2-50. The firm made Industrial Work Wear and during the '60s produced drainpipe-style jeans with the familiar black and green stitching up the side of the legs. The thick material for the work garments was heavy to handle. It was softened by rubbing with a carbolic type of soap then hit with a small metal hammer to make it softer and pliable becoming easier to get beneath the foot of the machine to do the stitching. They also made a range of boys' clothing under the name of "Abrovian": this included short trousers and corduroy jerkins. The workers were a happy crowd and the lines of machinists enjoyed their working days together.

Astin Bros. Ltd.

Manufacturers of
"ABROVIAN" FLANNELS for MEN
BOYS' KNICKERS and KIDDIE SHORTS
With the Snug Fit (patented) Waist Band
also
"ABRO" OVERALLS and all kinds of ARTISAN CLOTHING

FACTORIES
HEBDEN BRIDGE - - SOWERBY BRIDGE
and LUDDENDEN

Sewing Machinists, Astin's, c.1960. Taken at the side of Astin's premises off Burnley Road. L-R Front – Over shoulder, Marjorie Gannon (Linford), Valentina Fearnley (Caraluna), Christine Greenwood, Anne Higgins, Denise Poole and Anne Barnett.
Two girls behind: Valerie Clegg (Hitchcox) Joan Hodgson (Fullaway).
Back Row: Emmeline Pollard (Singleton) Elaine Barber, Jean Armitage (Marsh) Joyce Tetley (Hill) Dorothy Frane and lady with bag, Nora Wrigley.

The facilities for the tea making at break times were rather Spartan: the workers ate their food sitting at their machines; no canteen was provided. There was an old cooker and a tea urn, and during the morning and afternoon breaks a lady came to make tea and serve it to the workers. Sometimes a man would also call and sell them sandwiches. Any worker who was a smoker had to take their break downstairs outside the building.

Christine used to catch the Number 54, Boulderclough single-decker bus to get to her workplace on Burnley Road. It was known as the "Round-about bus" and was the only bus using the steep Quarry Hill on its route. This road is now extensively used and is really not suitable for the double-decker buses that use it. (Sowerby New Road is also another nightmare road to negotiate with a chicane and parked vehicles hindering drivers.)

As Christine waited for her bus at the stop below The Church Stile Inn, the bus would be visible over the wall as it left the terminus on at Boulderclough, at the road junction with Shield Hall Lane. The route ran around the Beechwood estate, down Quarry Hill, through Sowerby Bridge, left at Rochdale Road then left along Park Road into Beech Road, and right up Tuel Lane, turning round near the top. The bus would be packed with people going to work and the air was full of cigarette smoke and the aroma of the oily smell of the mills impregnated in the clothing the passengers wore!

The Bowers

The Bowers family were neighbours of my friend Christine Greenwood at 26 The Newlands for fifty-seven years; they lived in the house after moving from Nether-ends (lower end of the field) on Dean Lane. They were a well-educated family and avid readers of books, particularly Mrs Alice May Bowers. The two sons were William Granville, born in 1943 and Donald in 1945. Granville was educated at Sowerby Bridge Grammar School and later served in the Air Force, spending time in Aden. He died aged sixty-three in the Calderdale Hospital on the 16th April 2006. The Church Stile Inn collected money to give him a "proper" funeral, and also bought a bench in his memory, for customers to use. He had also been a regular at The Rush Cart pub.

Mr Bowers was a rather strange character: he would often talk to himself and was also hard of hearing. I remember seeing him at the bus stop opposite St Peter's Church with a carrier bag full of bread to feed the pigeons in George Square, Halifax. He also used to call Morecambe – "Morrycambee". Suffering from tuberculosis at one time, he lived in a tent in the garden to breathe in the fresh air. He was a ventriloquist and as the photographs illustrate had an assortment of dummies and paraphernalia to accompany his acts! He also used to perform at concerts held at Rooley Lane Chapel.

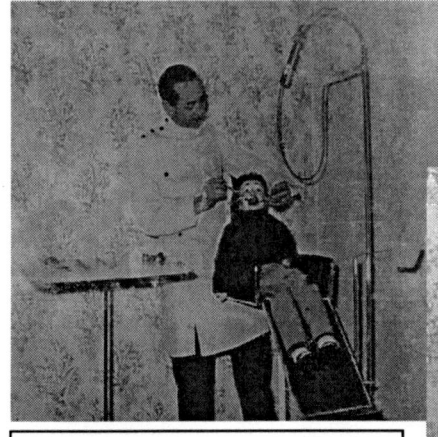

Mr Rothwell Bowers with the dummies and accessories used in his ventriloquist acts.

Mr Bowers was also a local inventor. He used to take some of his inventions to the Star pub and the customers would assess and try them out. He invented a type of coal fire grate, which was tested and then patented. It was designed so that the coals could not fall out of the grate. The fire was later used in the Tarren Houses that were built on The Newlands during the 1950s.

Sadly their home life became chaotic as the boys grew up. Alcohol played a large part of the family's decline and Donald, who had been struggling with depression for some time, and had unsuccessfully sought the help he needed from his Doctor, committed suicide. He ran down through the fields below our house in Pinfold Lane and onto the railway line to meet the on coming train. He was thirty-two years old; it happened on the day of the Queen's Silver Jubilee celebrations in June 1977. Christine Greenwood had organised a street party for the children on the estate; it was held on the grass island opposite her house. Christine heard on the Radio Leeds news that someone had been killed on the railway track, later learning that it was Donald.

Christine was a great help to Mrs Bowers: by the time there was just her and Granville in the house, things had deteriorated and there was no daily routine as Mrs Bowers' health declined. Christine made a Sunday lunch for Mrs Bowers for ten years and helped her by being a kind and considerate neighbour in many other ways.

The Star Inn

The Star Inn was built by the Jennings family in 1798; a Captain Jennings was the first landlord of the pub. His father Stephen Jennings was a provision dealer who at one time supplied the former Sowerby Workhouse at Bentley Royd in Sowerby New Road. When Captain Jennings died in 1800, the Star Inn passed on to his wife. She was to marry again ten years later to John Whiteley, also known as John Almighty. Several people in Sowerby were known by by-names at that time. When their son was born he also was named John.

John Whiteley was born on 25 March 1788 at Longbottom, Sowerby. He went into the woollen trade as his father John before him. He married Captain Jennings' widow, becoming the landlord of The Star Inn when he was about twenty-two years of age. He was quite well-educated and soon became a prominent person in the village. Serving as a representative of the township in various offices, much of his success was due to his enthusiasm and enquiring nature, even if this could be interpreted as being of a bombastic disposition. He was elected Constable for 1827. He "preached" from a "pulpit" (an old Post Boy's box) in an upper room at the pub. His ghost is reputed to haunt the Star Inn.

George Habergham (Tony Murphy's grandfather) was the landlord of the Star Inn during the 1920s. Tony's mother Florence and her sister Doris were born at the Traveller's Rest pub and grew up at the Star Inn. When she was a young girl his mother would sit in John Almighty's chair!

Bar Lounge, Star Inn, Sowerby, 1956/7
L-R: Mr Cox? Pat Dick, Doris Broadbent, Ethel Spence, Mrs Annie Bottomley & Mr Herbert Bottomley, Sylvia Spence & Irvine Gannon (later married)

The Star Inn was taken over during 1958/59 by Mr Frederick John Taylor and his wife Hilda; they came from Birkenhead. They were also helped in the pub by their daughter Patricia and son-in-law Malcolm Nobes, who also worked for Valentine's in Halifax as a joiner. They had come to Sowerby from Hoylake in Cheshire.

Star Inn, Sowerby, Pub outing to the Races, 1955/6
Back Row L-R: Peter Bohen, Jack Berry, Rear Tom? France,
Rear: (glasses) Howard Holroyd
Middle Row: Mavis Winkley (Edwards) ? Tom Exley, Rear Flat Cap? Glasses?
Rear: Pub Landlord Jo Kershaw, Ted Fairbrother ? Betty Kershaw (Landlady)
Front kneeling, ? Parrott, Harold Whippey, ?, Jim Jackson, Harold
Smithson; Front: David Kershaw (son of landlord/lady)

Malcolm found the picture of John Almighty in the attic at the pub. It was decided not to hang it up in the pub, so someone from Whittaker's Brewery took the portrait away. For a while it hung on the wall in one of the firm's offices. Later when the brewery closed, the painting was auctioned along with other items. This information quells any former stories of it being stolen; it later turned up on The Antiques Road Show from Arundel Castle in West Sussex on September 9th 2007. The painting is now owned by a couple and was valued by Philip Mould at £2,500; many local Sowerby folk would like to have the portrait reinstated in its former home. The couple have had some strange "happenings" since hanging the portrait in their home. At one time hearing Brahms' Lullaby emitting from a bedroom, then ceasing as they climbed the stairs to investigate! Visitors to their house also dislike the painting!

While the Taylors ran the Star Inn there was a man who travelled around on horseback, selling his paintings and sketches that he carried in his saddlebags. After tethering his horse to the drainpipe at the Star, the man would say, "I would like to partake of your best ale, Landlord, and a bucket of water for my trusty steed." There was concern that the drainpipe would be parted from the wall, but it remained intact. This caller was perhaps the local author from Todmorden called William Holt with his white horse Trigger. I found a copy of his book, *Trigger in Europe*, first published in 1966, in our loft. The pages were brown with age. I decided to read it and found that I couldn't put it down. Beautifully written and a huge achievement for man and horse, this book had many tender moments of the relationship between the animal and the rider!

Malcolm and Patricia left the pub during 1962 and her parents some time around 1963.

Star Inn, Sowerby, early 1920s. Licensees, George & Emily Habergham

Young neighbour Harold Smith with his dog, Clifford Habergham (eldest son) of the licensees and his mother Emily Habergham

The Star Inn was renamed the Rush Cart some years ago due to its connection with the Rushbearing Festival held annually in September. The present landlord Robert (Bob) Thompson took over at the pub on the 7th November 2003.

Sowerby Buses: Conductors and Drivers

Eric Bartholomew (Bart)

Eric Bartholomew was a long-serving bus conductor/driver for Halifax Corporation and later Metro; I visited him in his bungalow at Moorlands View, Sowerby on 15/07/09 to talk about his time working, "On the Buses".

Eric was born in 1928 and lived at Scar Head in Norland; he had been employed earlier as a joiner/cabinet maker at Tidswell's, situated on Wharf Street, Sowerby Bridge, and also at Leah's Joiners & Funeral Directors in Triangle. Here Eric also assisted with the laying out of bodies: not for the faint-hearted, I should imagine!

I first knew Eric when he was married to his late wife Audrey and lived at 39, The Newlands, Sowerby. He worked on the buses from 1955-1986, starting on the buses as a conductor and after about ten months he spent ninety hours in his own time with the Driving School Buses, learning to be a bus driver and the routes he would be using. His conductor for many years was Jim Perry who was known as Jim Boy: they were regulars on the Sowerby and Ripponden bus routes.

Eric (Bart) Bartholomew & Jim (Jim Boy) Perry, a regular team on the Sowerby bus route.

Mary Thorpe was regular conductress on the Sowerby buses; she was tall and slim with rimless glasses. Mary ran a "tight ship" or rather bus when she was taking the fares and dishing out the tickets! She knew her job inside out, you didn't mess with Mary! She could be rather aloof and certainly didn't stand any nonsense on the bus she was in charge of. On one occasion I was going to catch a bus to go to work in Halifax to start at 8-30am; I was still in my teens. There was a Sowerby "turn-back" bus pulled in on the end of The Newlands; I thought that I would get on it there rather than walk down to the bus stop opposite St Peter's Church. Mary was reclining on the side seat (this is where she also used to do her knitting): as soon as my foot trod onto the bus platform, she informed me that I could not board the bus. "Why not?" I asked her. "Because this is not an official bus stop, that is why." I felt rather humiliated, stepped off the bus and walked down to the official bus stop. (She would be perfectly in her rights doing this; it was a bit naïve of me thinking that Mary would allow anyone to board the bus there.)

When she collected my fare, some further comments were passed between us; I can't remember exactly what was said. I do remember telling her that she had no need to be so rude and that I would report her when I reached my destination in Halifax! Needless to say I didn't report her – she was a regular on my bus route and I certainly did not want to get on the wrong side of Mary!

Eric told me that Mary would always give assistance to a mother with a baby and pram when they were boarding or alighting from the bus. She would hold the baby whilst the mother dealt with the pram, never the other way round! Eric was once driving into Halifax with Mary working as the conductress; as they turned the corner to go down by the Town Hall, a pushchair rolled out from under the stairs and into the road! Mary rang the bell, jumped off the bus to retrieve the pushchair and they continued on their journey.

In later years the design of the buses changed and instead of the driver having a separate cab, he was now seated within the bus. The loss of having a conductor on the bus and the driver now issuing tickets to passengers as they board has several disadvantages. Young mums struggle to cope with baby, pram and perhaps another toddler; maybe, if lucky, another passenger offers to help them. The conductor would be on hand to assist with a smile, and also be aware of what was going on within the bus and could deal with any problems as they arose with passengers. They were also another pair of eyes when the bus needed to reverse into awkward places, giving instructions to the driver for the manoeuvre. When the buses struggled in the snow and on icy roads, the conductor would alight from the bus and scatter ashes under the wheels to get a grip and enable the bus to move forward without skidding and sliding. The cinders/ashes were kept in a box under the stairs at the rear of the bus, hopefully accompanied by a shovel. If not available, the wooden board that the conductor used to rest on when filling in his timesheets would be a substitute used to scatter the ashes around.

There were kind people along routes who would make the bus crews jugs and pots of tea for their snap and break times. Mrs Briggs from Haigh's Buildings provided jugs of tea that were taken on board and the contents consumed at the bus terminus at either Steep Lane or at Hubberton. Mrs Georgeson who lived in the cottage below the Post Office and Mrs Pickles at Sowerby Green across from the former "Old Green Chapel" also used to make pots of tea for the bus staff. One of her sons, Clarrie Pickles, also worked on the buses; the buses used to turn round and pull into the yard where they lived.

Ernest Mitchell

Industrial Road, Sowerby Bridge.

When Ernest started work on the buses in 1954 his pay was £5 basic, plus any overtime he worked. He used to drive to Hardcastle Crags on what were known as "Star Sundays": these were every thirteenth week on the rota. On that day staff earned double time and a half! His wife Pauline (Addy) and their two little girls would join his bus and whilst the other passengers

Ernest Mitchell at the lower end of Crossfield Bus Station, Halifax showing Broad Street behind. Rear of The Sportsman pub Upper Crown Street and the dome of the Nat West Bank.

Hardcastle Crags bus: Ernest with his wife Pauline.

enjoyed their free time in the Crags, the family would sit and eat the picnic that Pauline had prepared and packed for them.

During the '60s there were "Countryside Tours" available to the public. I remember that my mother used to enjoy going on these outings; they were popular and well supported on a Sunday afternoon. The single-decker buses left from Commercial Street in Halifax, and the outing usually lasted for about two hours. There were three routes locally: one of them went up Ripponden Bank, over to Scammonden, calling at the Brown Cow for passengers to refresh themselves with a shandy or with a glass of lemonade.

Ernest trained to become an instructor and used to teach from a classroom at the Skircoat Road Depot. He was complimented on his ability to teach by his many pupils who attended his classes and went on to become skilled bus drivers.

Ernest holding an instruction class for bus drivers at the Skircoat Road depot.

Driver training buses leaving the Bus depot on Skircoat Road, Halifax.

Ernest in conductor's uniform with his bus.

Ernest, happy at his work!

Les and Brian Crossley

Some time after speaking with Eric Bartholomew, I had the chance to "find" another bus worker whom I had known as a young girl whilst living here in Sowerby. The Crossley brothers were unidentical twins and lived at 32, The Newlands on the bottom side of the grass- and tree- planted island.

After some detective work and with help from another ex-bus driver, I was given the e-mail address of Les. He was now living in St Paul's Bay in Malta with his second wife Shirley, whom he had met in 1992. They married in July 1999 and after enjoying Malta for their holidays fell in love with the place and decided to retire there in June 2006.

Although Les and Brian were born in the village of Luddenden on the 27th of February 1940, Les has always regarded Sowerby with affection as the place where he grew up as a child and teenager before leaving for good in 1964. His elder sister Margaret was five years older than her twin brothers. Their parents were called Ernest and Elsie. Les was fair and slightly built while Brian was dark and stocky – unless you knew about them being twins you would never have guessed it!

Les attended Triangle School as a young boy. Leaving at the age of 11 he moved to Bolton Brow Boys' Secondary School for the next stage of education. He learnt to play the violin and was in the school orchestra. Eventually he became the leader of the violin section and remembers performing at concerts held in Sowerby Bridge at Prince's Hall.

He remembers the lovely summers of his childhood and playing with his friends, including Donald Hepworth, in the small woodland behind The Newlands at the bottom of the field where the Delph is, before the building of council houses at Rooley Banks and Rawson Wood sheltered accommodation.

Les left Bolton Brow Boys' School at 15 years old and in July 1955 joined his father working in a woollen mill, Sykes and Co. on Wakefield Road, Sowerby Bridge. He was a "mule-spinner", making warp and weft bobbins which then went onto another floor where his father was a loom-tuner. His wages were about £3-10-0 a week. Brain worked for a short time in the office at Siddall & Hilton's on Wharf Street in Sowerby Bridge, leaving after a short time to join them at the mill. When the twins were 18 years, old Brian decided to leave and work on the buses where the wages were better. Les also had a part-time job to supplement his income, working evenings at the Essoldo Cinema on Wharf Street in Sowerby Bridge as a projectionist. He worked there six nights a week; his working day started at 7-15am till 5-15pm at the mill; he would then call at the café on Wharf Street for a bite to eat, then start his shift at the cinema for 8pm. He finished around 10-45pm and 11-15pm: working these long hours provided the money to help pay for Les's motorbike. By now he was earning £5 a week at the mill and felt rather envious of Brian who was earning between £10 and £12 a week on the buses, so he decided to also work on the buses! He started working as a conductor during November 1958, later working as a driver in July 1961, staying until early 1963.

He covered most of the routes in the early days and after a while was able to choose a favourite route, Queensbury/Boothtown, which he then did for most of the time.

He enjoyed the work and getting to know regular passengers on the buses, having a smile and a chat with people made his job pleasurable.

Margaret his sister and her family had emigrated to Australia in December 1963. Les decided to follow in February 1964. He worked at a large steelworks in Port Kembla as a furnace-charger and was then promoted to "Rolling Mill Recorder", keeping records of all the work that was completed during that shift. Returning to England for a couple of years in May 1967, he married, then in November 1969 left yet again for Australia. He also worked as a bus driver "down under", returning to this country in December 1973.

A Bus Story from Les Crossley
Having been a busman from the age of 18 until my final retirement at the age of 65, I now have the time to look back and can vividly remember some of the many funny and maybe not-so-funny incidents that occurred.

Going back to about 1962, I clearly remember Graham, my conductor and myself, when one day during the week we were doing the run to Causeway Foot. Now, in those days, we used to have quite a bit of what we called "standing time" at the terminus.

A gentle old lady got on the bus and sat down, now me and Graham we also were sat inside the bus downstairs talking. We got into conversation with this lovely lady, who must have been about 80 years old. We had a good natter with her and then the time came when it was time to go, so Graham, who was a joker, had brought a white walking stick with him, so he helped me up from where I was sat and said, "Come on, it's time to go." He got hold of my arm and helped me to get off the bus and walked me round to the driving cab with the white stick. The lady – bless her – asked Graham "Is he OK to drive?" He told her, "Oh, don't worry – I have been with him almost 12 months now and he is a good driver."

Raymond Spencer's Memories

During January 2010 contact was made through The Book Case at Hebden Bridge with a former Sowerby resident called Raymond Spencer. He was born on the 7th March 1935 in the Halifax Royal Infirmary. His mother had gone there to visit his Grandmother who was at that time a patient there. His mother went into labour during her visit and gave birth to Raymond; there was no maternity unit in those days! She used to tell Ray that he started off life being an awkward little b---- and continued to be one throughout his life!

They lived at Walker Lane off Wakefield Road in Sowerby Bridge at the time. Later the family moved up to Sowerby when Ray was about three and a half years old to 34 Pollit Avenue, Beechwood. He lived there until getting married and has lived in Shelley, the other side of Huddersfield, for over 30 years. His uncle was Leslie Stead who featured in my book *Growing up in Sowerby ... and More*, pictured haymaking on page 25.

Leslie Stead and the farms

Leslie was married to Phyllis and they used to live on Kingsley Avenue in Beechwood. Leslie worked at Ball Green Farm up Rooley Lane at one time for Abraham Riley. An evacuee from London called Dennis Vinton lived with the Rileys for a time. He used to obtain tickets for the Young Farmers' dance for Raymond: they were in demand and hard to get hold of!

Smart guys with ties! L-R, Ray Spencer, Ronnie Taylor and evacuee Dennis Vinton. Taken at a dance held in the Prince's Hall, Hollins Mill Lane, Sowerby Bridge. c. 1950.

Raymond remembers loading the milk float up at Ball Green with milk churns when the horse, called Tommie, was suddenly startled by something and shied up and the consignment of milk teemed out into the yard. Raymond had the job of cleaning the spillage up. His uncle also was a helper some time later at Stones Farm along Dob Lane at the time my father used to keep animals there. Raymond as a young boy used to also help out on the farm where there were cows, a dozen pigs and some hens. There was a sheep kept occasionally, but they usually strayed and never returned.

This was the period when the Black Market was up and running rather successfully in the Sowerby area. Leslie Stead used to assist my father in dealing with meat when the demand was high during the war. They never "rustled" cattle: this did happen and Ray remembers a report in the *Courier* about a case involving Slates Delves Farm at Blackshaw Head. Regular trips to hotels on the west coast to supply the hoteliers were made by my father during the Black Market days. This would be of much consternation to the local Health Inspector at the time, a man called Mr Eric Foster. He was the chief Public Health inspector in Sowerby Bridge before the Second World War and also qualified in clean air and smoke control.

There was a small dairy where Raymond would help to churn cream in a wooden machine, turning until his arm ached, or in his own words, "Till me arms nearly dropped off." During haymaking one time he was wearing sandals on his feet when he stuck a pitchfork through his foot. He was taken on to hospital in my father's Humber car with his uncle Leslie, was cleaned up and no stitches were required. As the pair came out of the building his uncle gave him a clip around his ear hole and scolded him, "A'v lost 'alf a day's 'eymakin cos a tha bloo----- stoopidity, if tha'd 'ad thi clogs on tha'd 'a bin alreight, tha'l a'ta work late." His uncle did give him a little more cash though for the extra time put in at the farm. Raymond remembers Joyce King from Boulderclough featured in my previous book on page 26: Ray told me that her white shorts attracted attention as he and his friends cycled past the haymaking fields, causing many a bike wobble as they turned their heads to get a better look at the glamorous worker in the field!

School Days
Raymond attended St Peter's Infants' School in Sowerby. The teachers then were Mrs Crossley, Miss Taylor, Miss Edwin, Mrs Mitchell, Mr Albrighton (later called up for service in the Army) and the Head was Mr Hollas. The caretaker was Thomas Brown who was also a long serving bellringer at St Peter's Church.

At 14 years of age the boys and girls then in the top class would leave to start working; this later changed when the leaving age was raised to 15. Anyone who sat and passed their eleven-plus examination went to the Sowerby Bridge Grammar School on Albert Road. Girls who failed went on to attend Sowerby

New Road Secondary School and the boys to Bolton Brow Secondary Modern School. Something that puzzled the children in his class was the fact that Sheila Addey, a pupil in the same class, had her uncle in the top class at the same school. The children found this rather confusing and difficult to understand!

The Addey family were the owners of a large fish and chip restaurant at the end of Station Road. Later they ran a fish shop at The Nook. Station Road was at one time a private road, and once a year a chain used to be hung across it by the London, Midland and Scottish Railways. Raymond cannot remember when this ceased to be done.

Ray's dad was a regular at the Church Stile pub when Joe Coley was the landlord. If his Dad failed to be in the pub half an hour after opening time, Joe would send his son Terry with a crate of Whitaker's beer down to his bungalow in Beechwood. It was Ray's task to return the empties later to the pub!

The King's Head Pub which stood in Town Gate above the Alms Houses later became the Church Institute. School dinners were provided here at one time. When sausage and mash was the menu of the day, occasionally they ran out of sausages! Children who had "missed out" had their names written down by a teacher to enable them to go to the front of the queue the next time the dish was on the menu. School meals were later served in the school hall (most likely when the building was demolished).

The Cubs and Scouts meetings were held in the Church Institute. The vicar at that time was called Mr. C.E.E. Glasgerdine who was vicar at St Peter's from 1940-5. This gentleman only had one arm. He was popular with the youngsters and involved them with the Church, resulting in some of the older residents feeling somewhat neglected. Ray sang in the church choir where Alfred Nicholl was the choirmaster and organist. A small concrete pond was built in the vicarage garden which was then situated down Lane Ends – which leads into Triangle from Dean Lane and is on the bend on the right. Many of the young boys including Raymond learnt to swim in the pool. The swimming baths in Sowerby Bridge were not open at that period and the nearest one was at Elland. During the 1960s a house was bought in Sowerby for use as a vicarage and the old vicarage was sold and renamed The Glebe House.

Mr and Mrs Hollas lived in the School House at the rear of the school. They had a garage lower down Back Lane. Mr Hollas used it for his car and during the war the car was laid up on blocks, not in use. Raymond was about five years old when one night the garage caught fire. The vehicle and the garage were destroyed as a result. It was rumoured about the village that perhaps it had been an arson attack.

"The Village"

Below the school and down Back Lane and through a stile was a small square of land. It was known as "The Village": grassless, it was an area of soil erosion and this gave the impression of sand. Children used to play here, their Dinky wagons and cars making "roads" in the sand. The older boys would play cricket here and sometimes the ball would be hit and land in the field beyond their play area. The farmer who owned it was called Mr Burton. If he caught any of the boys in his field he would remove his leather belt and whack their bottoms with it! If a girl was caught she would be summoned to appear before Mr Hollas the head teacher to be reprimanded. No one ever complained about their treatment: it was just part of growing up.

St Peter's Church, about 1906, showing the area known as "the Village" Through the stile at the front of the picture, children used this area as a playground.

Wartime

Raymond remembers the air raid shelters being built on land given by Colonel and Mrs Stansfeld. This was at the top of a field at the Dean Lane end. The excavator arrived and was driven up the road in front of the School House, into the field and started to dig out the shelter. When they were dug out, the soil that had been excavated was piled up on top of the shelters, leaving only the air vents showing. At the bottom side of the shelters, land was later dug over to make an allotment where vegetables were grown. This was started by the teacher Mr Charlie Albrighton before he was drafted into the Army; maybe the produce grown was given out to the old folk in the village or used in the preparation of school dinners?

Ray was engrossed and lost track of the time as he watched the digger at work, when he suddenly felt a sharp pain on his bottom, as his mother angrily dragged him from the wall! She was cross and had come searching for him, as school lessons had finished at 3-45 pm and it was now 6-30 pm. There was no tea that evening for the naughty boy!

Ray recalls a Mickey Mouse type of gas mask; they were made out of pink rubber and had two round glass porthole type windows with a pink tongue sticking out at the front! The lads discovered that a rather disgusting noise could be made by blowing into the mask rather than breathing in, much to their amusement! The masks were distributed to the public from Prince's Hall on Hollins Lane.

Mrs Crossley's classroom housed a dapple-grey rocking horse (several schools in our area had them). When he saw it some years later the poor horse was looking rather tatty, the red saddle and reins plus the horse's mane had all disappeared. This was quite distressing to Ray: when it was used by the children of his schooldays, the rocking horse was treated with respect as if it was a real horse. He remembers riding our rocking horse Silver at 32 Town Gate; he was allowed a ride on it after asking permission from my mother and brother David.

The war had now started and Mr Albrighton had left school to serve in the Army. About this time a new teacher arrived at the school: she was called Mrs Gravis. Other arrivals were children who had been evacuated from areas likely to be bombed during the war. Mrs Gravis used to bring groups of these children to Sowerby to be accommodated with local families. Mrs Gravis would arrive with the children and stay for a few months, then leave and return with more children at a later date. Our late next door neighbour Mrs Trixie Fox at "The Curatage" in Pinfold Lane told me years ago that she put up child evacuees during the war. Some of these children were poorly clothed after losing much in the bombings that had taken place. Some of them were from Hull and lived in poor housing near to the docks. These children were difficult "to get on with" for a while as some of them were suffering from traumatic shock as it would be called today. In those days they were just unfortunate in what they had experienced during the war.

Ray and his friends used to play in the small wooded plantation that was situated on Dean Lane next to where Austin Mitchell lives at Longfield and where the housing estate now ends. They played games involving "sword fights" and Robin Hood and made swings among the trees. Imagination was used by the children, and in a place where you could be concealed and hidden from view, so many games and adventures could be played out. One day the children found an empty old rusting oil drum and decided to put someone inside it and then hit the drum with sticks. (Ray's words: "the simple pleasures of the working poor.") The group of about six boys were taken by surprise as the din they created had attracted the attention of the local bobby, a rather large man called PC Telford. "You lot come 'ere," he requested: no one thought about running away. "You are making too much noise," he said, "Now get off home." Swinging his heavy cape he caught Ray on the forehead, cutting it and drawing blood. Returning home and feeling a little scared as PC Telford was a drinking friend of his grandfather's, his dad inquired, "What's tha done to thi een?" Ray replied, "Oh nowt. Bobbie Telford hit me with his cape." With that his father gave him a clip and the lad was lucky to get his supper that evening.

Another play area was the quarry situated in Sowerby New Road above Beechwood on the lefthand side of the road. Owned by the council, grit and chippings were kept here, also the old-fashioned triangular shaped snowplough which used to be pulled by horses. The lads used to secure a rope to a tree above the quarry and swing out high above the ground like Tarzan, cinema hero of the time! Unused for many years the council built a detached property called Quarry Rise. It accommodates several young adults with learning difficulties.

Games and handicrafts

"Fishing": Garden Party Game at The Stansfeld's, Field House, Dean Lane, Sowerby, 1950s.

Garden Parties were held at Field House along Dean Lane where local land owners the Stansfelds lived. Ray asked Mrs Stansfeld if he could have a sail in the rowing boat on the boating lake in the grounds. It was one old penny a ride, the lake was in fact quite small but to a young child appeared to be huge. There were stalls and games to play at these events, "Pin the Tail on the Donkey",

Hoopla, Bar Skittles and a type of Coconut Shy. This one was slightly different as the stands for the balls were the cardboard rolls that were inside toilet rolls. The balls were woollen pom-poms that the children used to make in school. Milk bottle tops in those days were made of cardboard to fit the wider necked bottles of the time. A hole was made and two tops put together and old wool wound round and round until the centre hole was filled up. The teacher would then cut around the outer edge of the circle, tie the centre and slide the cardboard off. Fluff up the wool and you have a woollen ball or pom-pom.

At school the girls did something called French Knitting (which has been done for more than a century). This was done on a wooden cotton bobbin. I remember having one of these given as a Christmas present: the bobbin had a painted face on and the "body" was coloured orange to look like a doll. Four small nails with heads on were knocked into the top at one end and the wool passed around the nails and cast off in sequence like knitting, by using a small hooked type implement. As you continued, the "worm" of wool became longer and eventually came out of the hole in the bottom of the bobbin. When enough knitting was completed, the worm was laid flat and coiled round like a rope and stitched to keep in place, to make a woollen coaster or tablemat.

The Kerridge Family

I have known the Kerridge family all my life; they lived near to us in Queen Street. We attended the same chapel, Sowerby Congregational known as the "Old Green", situated above the Star Inn (Rushcart) at the junction of Well Head Lane and Dob Lane. John is ten years older than me and has interesting accounts of his childhood and later life. He has kindly allowed me access to his writing and the following details are from his memoir.

Nos. 1, 2 and 3, Queen Street, Sowerby, 1910. John's Aunt Susan lived for 91 years at No. 1 – she is 3rd from the left with sisters Janet and Julia. In the doorway are Emily and Rachel Kerridge. The Crossley family lived at No. 2 and the Whiteley and Thomas families at No. 3. Courtesy of Dr John A. Hargreaves.

John's Memories

I was born on the 1st May 1933 at 2, Queen Street, Sowerby, in a mid-terrace stone house facing over the Calder Valley. It consisted of two bedrooms and two rooms downstairs, a keeping cellar and a "coal hole". Downstairs there was a kitchen-cum-living room at the back, and at the front was the sitting room which was usually reserved for weekend use only.

The kitchen comprised a table, sideboard, a sewing machine (folded down) seats and a buffet under the table. There was a covered washtub stand which Dad had made so that the rubber-rollered wringer could be clamped onto it on washdays, enabling Mum to take the washing straight out of the tub and wring it out, collecting the water back in the tub; this stand doubled as a small worktop the rest of the week.

There was a large cupboard in the corner housing a stone sink (sometimes called a slopstone) with a single cold tap which supplied fresh spring water from an underground tank in Well Head fields, belonging to our landlord Mr. Rawson. For hot water a kettle had to be boiled on a gas ring in the hearth or balanced on the open fire.

Next to the sink cupboard was the black-leaded range, which consisted of, on the left a fireside oven, in the centre the fire grate, and on the right a water boiler. To get the oven hot, the main flue from the grate was restricted, and a sliding metal plate was pulled out to divert the hot gasses underneath and behind the oven. The same applied to the water boiler on the other side: there was no tap on the boiler, so to get the hot water out a lading or ladling can was used. The boiler was also filled using this method.

The fire was not at floor level but about two foot up, allowing the ashes to drop underneath, making it easy to shovel them up in the morning. The lighting of the fire involved the use of a draw tin and newspaper, the drill being to light the fire, then put up the draw tin and newspaper to get maximum draught to the underside of the fire. When the fire was blazing merrily the paper and draw tin were quickly removed; occasionally the newspaper caught fire. Most people didn't have a draw tin; instead they used the broad hearth shovel. Both methods could prove rather dangerous!

In the hearth of the fireplace was the single burner gas ring, fed from a tap and rubber hose from the side of the lefthand cupboard: this and the fire which had a hob attached were the only daily means of making a meal, apart from Wednesday which was baking day. To the right of the "cooker/fire/water-boiler unit" was another built-in cupboard that had all the food and daily crockery necessary for our family of five. The room was illuminated by a single gas light in the middle of the ceiling. This may sound rather primitive today but it gave a good light and also contributed to the heating of the room, which despite the draughts from the cellar and room doors was always cosy.

The sitting-room at the front of the house contained a piano, which Mum played when the occasion arose, a grandfather clock (my family heirloom) and a three-piece suite. This room was only used at weekends and Christmas party time.

The front bedroom held a double bed for Mum and Dad, and my single bed with a screen around it, in a corner. The back bedroom had a double bed for my sisters Brenda and Margaret. Both rooms also had wardrobes.

As the house had no electricity, the routine at bedtime was to light a taper (like a very thin candle about 9 inches long) from either the fire or from the gas mantle, and take it upstairs to light a candle by the side of the bed. This may perhaps sound a little dangerous today, but we thought nothing of it! Once I wired up the cellar for light by a small switch, a battery and a 2.5 volt bulb: this didn't provide much light but was a start!

We had no inside toilet or bathroom; the bath was hung on a nail in the cellar for Friday evening use, and the toilet was on the end of the yard. Aunties Susan, Rachel and Janet living next door to us had a bathroom installed after the war; we never had either bathroom or toilet in the house, using the toilet outside until Margaret moved out to live in Pinfold Lane and join her friend Margaret Jowett. The unpleasant task of daily emptying the chamber pots or jerries had to be carried out. This was always Mum's job. She emptied them into an enamel bucket, washing them out, and then emptying the bucket down the outside drain in the road.

The toilet outside was a relic of the Victorian era. It was situated on the end of the yard in a purpose-built block; we entered the building and our toilet was on the left through a wooden plank door. It consisted of a well-scrubbed wooden seat with a large hole in the middle, which was a straight drop into an earth soak-away; it was always draughty when visiting due to ill-fitting doors of the midden to which the toilet was vented. There were no dustbins so everything which wouldn't burn on the fire was thrown through the wooden doors adjacent to the toilet door into the main body of the midden. The block served five or six families and must have been quite a health hazard! The council used to come about once a month to shovel out the contents into a special horse-drawn cart which was hopefully leak-proof! This was not a healthy job to do but it always smelled better after the men had been, as they spread their brick-coloured powdered disinfectant around! We always knew when Dad was in there as he took the newspaper with him: not to read as there was no light – he sat there tearing up the paper into useable sized "toilet tissue", and this was then pushed onto a nail in the wall for easy accessibility. Every now and then we had a pleasant surprise when we found some tissue paper hung there, usually taken from some oranges bought from our local greengrocers (oranges used to be individually wrapped in tissue paper). The process may not sound hygienic but it was the done thing in the days of "waste not want not". The toilet block was kept locked; the key was attached to a cotton bobbin usually hanging behind the cellar door.

There were other types of toilets around the village: my friend Ronnie Holt had a two-hole toilet, one for adults and the other for children, although they only used the larger one. They also had a modern type of waste disposal, a large bucket which was emptied each week; there was only one bucket hence the use of only one hole!

Across Queen Street from our house was a three-quarter acre field; this was Dad's hen pen. He rented this from Jimmy Greenwood at Town Farm.

It consisted of a large hut, which in the early years of the century was the Sowerby Brass Band practice room. There was a penny-operated gas meter installed which he used, connecting a gas supply into his workshop, a lean-to next to the band hut. The contents of this hut were, for as long as I can remember, three rows of hen battery cages, never used for their proper purposes, but only as "clocking boxes" for broody hens.

Mr Ernest Kerridge in his rented hen-pen field. Across the valley, Burnley Road is visible below housing on the right. 1960/61

Dad worked at the Sowerby Bridge Gas Works off Wakefield Road, Sowerby Bridge, working a shift system: his hours were noon-8pm one week, 8pm-4am another and 4am-noon. This was a six-day week, working a different shift each week. Any spare time was spent in his workshop and with his poultry.

The workshop was a large shed which had a dirt floor. There was a bench with drawers and a vice; on one side were two egg incubators, originally powered by oil, later converted by Dad to gas; there was also a gas light. He spent many evenings working in there, and was quite skilled at making old boots into clogs: these he used at work. During the war he also made ends meet by producing various toys, blackboards and easels, hoop-la, a garage for myself, sewing-boxes for my sisters, and made a variety of things for other folk. He often had a friend sitting with him for company: he was called Walker Barrett and he lived in nearby King Street.

Dad built next to the workshop a log lean-to shed for his hens. He hatched a set of chickens every year, reared them and kept them for two years when they were then sold for the table. We were never short of food during the war; a little farther down the field was the goose shed, which had about six residents every year until Christmas arrived! (Mrs Fox at The Curatage used to order one.) At the bottom of the field was another large "Apex" hut used for more hens; this was a distance to walk so he tried to keep most of the hens nearer the top of the field as all food and water had to be carried to them. In the field there were also three rearer huts and two more "Apex" huts belonging to my aunties.

The field and workshop were used by me to the utmost: the workshop for my bicycles and a go-cart – my Dad made it, it was unique in that it only had three wheels (old pram wheels were difficult to get during the war). The sloping field was ideal for sledging during the winter; it was ideal for burying treasure also; there are still farthings buried there. Later I was to have my own shed to keep and breed rabbits in, these were another source of meat during the war. There was also a bench and an old vice; it was in this shed that my pals and I had our first attempt at smoking. We rolled short lengths of string onto cigarettes on an acquired Rizla machine, lit up and never did it again – they were horrible!

The hen huts led to the occasional extra spending money, as they frequently needed cleaning out, not a pleasant job but I had to do it! Every year the hut roofs had to be tarred and all the woodwork on the Apex huts had to be creosoted. Doing this job in strong sunshine was unpleasant as the creosote that was used came straight from the gas works and if it was splashed onto the skin it burned!

At the top of Queen Street there was an allotment garden that belonged to my three aunts, Rachel, Janet and Susan, who lived next door to us at No 1 Queen Street; this provided some of our summertime supply of fresh fruit and vegetables. In the corner of the garden was a lean-to shed – this was used as a potting shed and also doubled up as a wash kitchen. In one corner there was a "set pan" under which a fire would be lit to heat the water it contained to boil the washing, and also to heat water to be ladled out into a Peggy tub for the clothes to be possed (with a posser – this was usually made of copper shaped like an upturned bowl with a wooden handle attached) and rubbed clean on a rubbing board. These were given a new use in the later days of skiffle groups, providing "music" when thimbles were worn over fingertips and the wavy metal board played, producing a distinctive noise to accompany the other improvised instruments. After the various stages of doing the washing were completed it had to be carried back some distance to be hung out on a line across Queen Street! (Weather permitting.) Dad was also a keen angler and family holidays were planned to coincide with the Annual Sea Angling Festival held at Bridlington every September – he was a frequent prizewinner!

* * * * * * * *

[John was first a cyclist moving later onto motorcycles, accumulating 50 years of experience and mechanical knowledge of the various machines he owned and having the ability to re-build a machine and carry out repairs, etc. His friends Barry Copley and Alan Ford were also keen motorcyclists. Barry has lived in Ghana at one time and grew pineapples for a living!

John worked at Wright Electric Motors Ltd, Halifax as an Electrical Engineer. Later he was called up to do his National Service from 1954-1956 in the Royal Air Force.

During 1958 John was now working in Elland for Wrights; it was here that he met Vera who was working in a local shop. They started courting and Vera soon became John's navigator on their motorbike excursions. After a meal at the "Hong Kong" restaurant in Halifax on 11th April 1960, they became engaged to be married; the ceremony was held at Elland Wesleyan Chapel on the 1st July 1961 and their two weeks' honeymoon was spent in France and Italy. They travelled there on John's Norton motorbike, a remarkable journey to undertake!]

* * * * * * * *

Around 1960/61 Vera and I heard that Jimmy Greenwood had a cottage to rent on his Little Wood Lane farm (off Pinfold Lane); we inquired about the rent he was asking and a weekly sum of seven shillings and sixpence was agreed upon: we bought our own rent book! On receipt of the key we spent some time decorating and furnishing the place. The cottage consisted of one up and one down with a small cellar, and in Jimmy's own words a slopstone at t'top o't cellar steps! There was also an outside unlit toilet.

John & Vera Kerridge in their rented cottage, Wood Lane, Sowerby. 1960/1.

Vera was now expecting our first child which was due in September 1961. As time passed Vera was growing in size and now unable to ride pillion on my motorbike, so a sidecar had to be found. After making inquiries I bought an almost new one from my pal Barry Copley, it was a Canterbury Carmobile, *child, adult* with sidecar wheel brake: it cost £110. After some trouble fixing it, it served us well for a few years.

Motorbike & Sidecar with baby Tracy inside! Parked at the end of the drive in Wood Lane.

69

The winter of 1963 brought a severe snowfall: in late January to mid- February the lane to our cottage became drifted up solid with snow. The council came to clear it, only for the same thing to happen again! The combination during this time stayed at the top of the lane, as it was impossible to get it out, once the lane was full of snow.

Heavy snow, Wood Lane; St Peter's Church rear left, Church Terrace rear right.

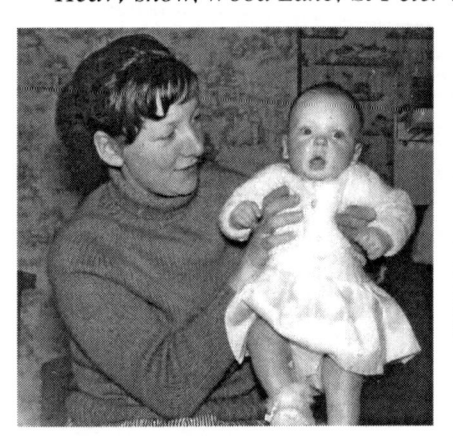

Vera decided to take up sledging as a way of getting back down home with the shopping and baby Tracy Frances who had been born on September 27th 1962. (John and Vera had three children: Tracy Frances, Peter John born 19th May 1964 and Victoria Jane, 25th February 1971.)

Vera & Baby Tracy, 1962

During 1966 we heard that the demolition of the old Providence Methodist Chapel in Town Gate was to commence and three terrace houses to be built on the site. We made some inquiries and discovered that the end houses were priced at £2,050 and the middle house for £1,950. These prices suited our budget as a 5% deposit would be £95: we could then become property owners! We took the plunge and paid our deposit on plot number 3; we would have liked number 1 plot with an adjacent drive, but this had previously been sold. It turned out later that we had the opportunity to buy a drive width on our end thus giving us access to both drives, our garage being on the shared drive. The land we bought was available after the demolition of the row of houses above the former chapel. We moved into our new house in late November 1966 and still live there.

****

[John later worked at Churchill Redman as a small parts inspector, and later at Gordon Sudworth, and finally at Appleyard Fuel Services of Leeds until he retired in May 1998.]

Vera Kerridge (Shaw)
Taken from Vera's memoirs.

Vera was born in Elland in 1935, at a house called "Sundial House". When she was about three years old, the family moved to a brand-new council house on the Elland Lane Estate. She began dancing about that time, although she wasn't keen on it and didn't start again until she was 10 years old. Whilst still at school she became involved with Sunday school concerts and also performing at Sunny Vale Pleasure Gardens during the summer time. Concerts were organised by the dancing school run by husband and wife team Norman Teal and Mildred Crossley. The Langdale Rooms in Elland is where Vera's dancing class was held although she has memories of having lessons earlier at Mildred's home. It was at the dancing school that Vera first met a very young Roy Castle. When Vera started to dance professionally she lost touch with Roy for several years, when he was called up to do his national service.

Roy Castle 1947. Young entertainer!

In the late '40s Miss Crossley took over the Queen's Theatre at Cleveleys outside Blackpool; from then on things became "professional". The older dancing girls who had left school were taken to appear in shows put on at The Queen's. The younger girls carried on with concerts under the supervision of Connie Hamer (sister of Derek) who was a wonderful dancer.

Vera was a pupil at Elland Grammar School and on reaching the age of 15 decided that she wanted to leave school. After discussions with her parents she got her own way and was ready to "go" if called upon to join the dancers!

A telegram arrived from Norman Teal, the manager, requesting Vera to pack a bag and join the show at Darlington; the summer season had ended and they were now on tour.

Vera was rather disappointed that she was only needed for a week to fill in for a girl who had a sprained ankle. Her appetite had now been whetted; the show was called "Happiness Ahead", in which Roy Castle was starring. The pantomime season began for Christmas 1950, "Goldilocks and the Three Bears" produced by Jack Gillam, who was based in Manchester. He approached Mildred when he needed a chorus line for one of his shows. Roy Castle played "Baby Bear" as he was small. The bears performed a speciality act before the finale, this involved Baby Bear performing an acrobatic movement which Roy was unable to do! This was when Vera who was the same height became a stand-in for Roy and completed the acrobatic performance, the audience thinking that it was Roy inside the bear suit!

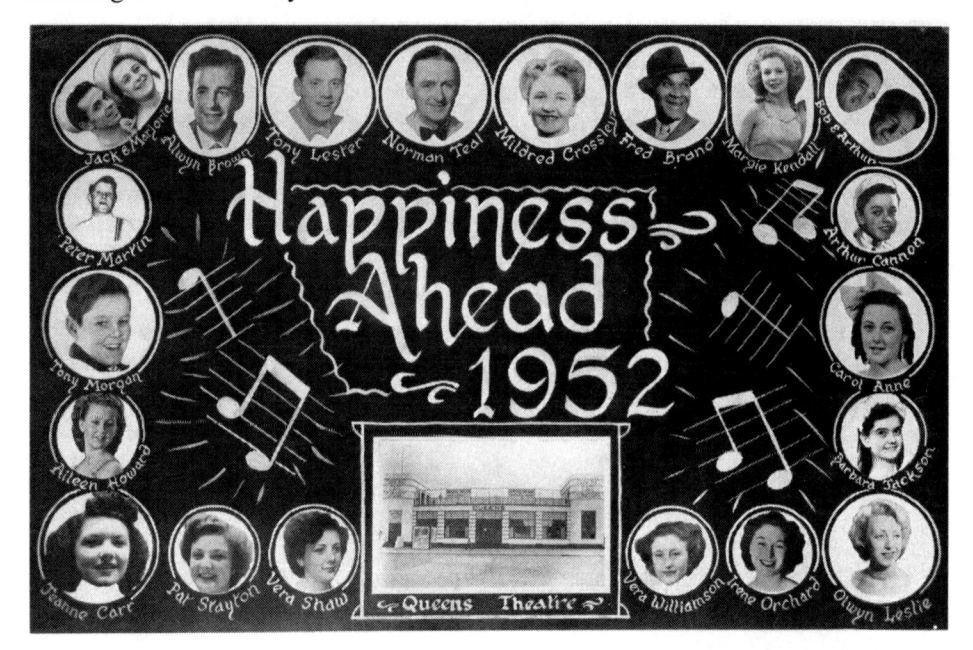

[Poster: Happiness Ahead 1952 — Queens Theatre. Cast: Jack & Marjorie, Alwyn Brown, Tony Lester, Norman Teal, Mildred Crosley, Fred Brand, Margie Kendall, Bob & Arthur, Peter Martin, Arthur Cannon, Tony Morgan, Carol Anne, Aileen Howard, Barbara Jackson, Jeanne Carr, Pat Stayton, Vera Shaw, Vera Williamson, Irene Orchard, Olwyn Leslie]

The group went on tour with "Happiness Ahead"; the show had the same title but had a changed routine with songs and sketches. They gave three shows every week plus matinees if the weather was wet! This ran for two summer seasons at Cleveleys, 1951/52.

This was followed by working on one of Jack Gillam's revues on tour, then back to "Goldilocks" panto, 1952/53. Vera then worked for a production company called Richards and Hicks: this was run by Dickie Richards and Edwin Hicks. The first show was called "Girls, You're Gorgeous". Touring was hard work: the girls would leave home by train on a Sunday; their carriage would have been reserved for them. They were given a list of "digs" where to stay if these hadn't been pre-booked for them. Some of these varied between good, bad and awful! The girls usually managed to find self-catering accommodation; this involved paying for the room, buying their own food and the landlady cooking it for them! This cost between 15 and 30 shillings in old money, 75p and £1-50 today. The girls put 10 or 15 shillings (50p and 75p) into a "catering purse" and took turns at doing the shopping!

The pantomime for 1953/4 was "Sinbad the Sailor"; Edwin wrote the whole production including the comedy. Vera's role was "Palmyra the Dancing Girl" doing some comedy in this part alongside Tony Dalton who was the top-billed comedian. This involved having a custard pie in her face: the audience screaming with laughter as it was unusual for the glamour girl to be on the receiving end!

Pantomimes lasted for six weeks; a week was then taken out, and back to rehearse for a new revue. With just a week to put everything together and perhaps eight routines to learn, this was a hectic time. Leaving on the Sunday by train, there would be a wardrobe rehearsal on the Monday with three morning sessions or daily if required! Another show, "Kiss Me Goodnight, Sergeant Major" included songs from both World Wars; this was very patriotic and the audience often cried whilst applauding loudly. "Girlie" shows were performed; these included topless nudes who in those days were forbidden to move. The local authorities would intervene if these rules were broken. Some theatres would not entertain nudity; Leeds City Varieties did allow them. One of the sleaziest theatres Vera remembers was Collin's Music Hall, Islington; the audience was full of old men! The girls were paid about £2 per week extra to appear "nude". Vera wasn't among the girls doing this.

The following were some of the "Girlie Shows":

"Cabaret de Paris" (pronounced Paree!); "Briefs"; "This Year's Blushes;" "How Naughty Can You Get?"; "Nice Goings On"; "Exotique" and "Gay Paree" (when "gay" meant lively and bright). All sounds a little corny today, but going back to the '50s this would be quite "daring".

Chorus Line: L-R, Jo, Vi, Cindy, Irene, Kathie, Vera, Babs, Beryl.

After appearing in "Sinbad", Vera knew everyone's part! When Edwin went off for a week to see his other panto productions, Vera was left in charge of rehearsals. She performed in almost every small town in England, though never Scotland. Wales and Belfast were included where the nudes were taboo! The American air base at Burton Wood welcomed the troupe like royalty. Here they received gifts of nylon stockings, Peter Stuyvesant cigarettes, chocolates and other goodies that were unavailable in England at that time.

River Boat scene from a touring revue.

Between February 20th 1956 and December 10th the tour for "Exotique" had forty bookings throughout Great Britain including The Palace Theatre in Halifax on 23rd July; moving next on to Belfast on the 13th August to perform at the Empire theatre for a three-week booking: this was a rare treat for the girls.

During October the group would return to the same theatre again, this time with a new show. This would be rehearsed whilst still on tour with the current one. By this time Vera had become "head girl" of the troupe. By the late 1950s, theatres had begun to close down, maybe a result of the television coming into our lives, making work difficult to find. Edwin came up with the idea of an all- girl Skiffle Group to work the clubs. Vera and her friend Jo with a couple of other girls formed "The Slick Chicks"; the group did perform in a few clubs but they didn't last long as performing in clubs is different as there are no foot lights to separate the performers from the audience and the girls didn't care for this.

The Slick Chicks Skiffle Group: L-R, Jo Hurd (mother of Michaela Strachan, the TV presenter) Vera Kerridge (Shaw) Sally Kelly and Nan Dawn

Sadly Vera's father was now very ill and the panto of 1957/58 was the last one that she would perform in as a professional dancer. She wanted to be at home at this difficult time. She "went out in style" as she was asked to fill the shoes of the Principal Boy Sinbad after she had failed to return after a weekend home visit. The show was at the Playhouse Theatre, Bury St Edmonds on 13th January 1958. Vera describes it as, "one of the best weeks of my life"

Her family decided to take on a tiny shop in Elland; they rented it and sold a few groceries, bread, sweets and cigarettes. Vera ran it and made sandwiches for the workers from the nearby mills and factories. It was here that she was to meet John Kerridge her future husband.

Later in her life, in 1994, Vera became involved with "The Calderdale Support Group" formed to raise cash for the Roy Castle Lung Cancer Foundation. Twelve million pounds was required to build the research centre in Liverpool. The group did various events of fund-raising, coffee morning, bring-and-buy sales and raffles. Then an idea to do some sponsored tap-dancing arose, and from these small beginnings the "Tapathon" was born in 1977. It was Derek Hamer, the leader of the small group of tap dancers who thought up the idea.

After Roy's death in 1994 his wife Fiona laid the foundation stone for the new building to which the group were invited.

Schools and dancing schools were invited from areas to perform a 20-minute session each; if enough entrants were found perhaps they could tap all day. Sponsorship would then raise money for the cause. Halifax Leisure Centre at North Bridge has been the home of the annual Tapathon for several years, raising amounts of £500 in one day to £10,000 the following year. The number of dancing schools taking part every year varied between 14 and 18 and up to 300 dancers taking part from age 3 to 83!

Coverage was given by local press and television. Over the years "The Calderdale Support Group" has raised more than £149,000 (mostly at the Tapathon) for Roy's Foundation Centre in Liverpool and has been used in research for the earlier detection of lung cancer.

The fifteen Tapathons and two previous years of other fundraising have totalled £243,000.

*Jan 2000 Tapathon, North Bridge Leisure Centre, Halifax.
Fiona Castle centre, Vera on her right.*

Margaret Kerridge

Margaret had many years' connection with the Brownies and Guides. She first attended meetings held at Sowerby Congregational Chapel (Old Green) at the junction of Well Head Lane and Dob Lane. Her Aunt Susan and a lady called Muriel Smith used to take the Guide meetings at one time; a pack for Brownies was formed in later years.

Margaret started as a helper with the Brownies when she was about 15/16 years old.

The girls enjoyed lots of walking around the Sowerby hills and country lanes, and also had occasional day trips. Margaret was Brown Owl at Sowerby for 30 years and to mark her dedication and achievement a presentation was arranged for the last meeting of the pack to be held at Old Green which was due to close on 2nd December 1979.

Mrs Elizabeth Hull, District Commissioner presents Margaret with her long service award.

The Divisional County Commissioner Mrs Elizabeth Hull presented her with a new award, a silver Guide badge on a blue background. Margaret was the second person to receive it for long service in Yorkshire.

Margaret, who was born on the 17th November 1928, lived at 2, Queen Street, Sowerby for 62 years, eventually leaving to move in with her friend Margaret Jowett at Pinfold Green during April 1992. They are known to everyone as "the two Margarets".

Margaret Jowett, Margaret Kerridge and Mrs Hull

Both were Sunday School teachers at Old Green for many years and worked tirelessly in the running of the chapel and the events that were held there. When the chapel closed on December 2nd 1972, the two friends later began to attend Steep Lane Baptist Chapel. Margaret Jowett continued to write her interesting accounts of "From my window" for the chapel magazine, the extensive panorama viewed from their rear window providing lots of material throughout the seasons for Margaret to record.

Margaret Kerridge was baptised at Steep Lane Chapel on the 5th September 2010. The service conducted by the Rev. Jane Powell was attended by Margaret's family and friends, gathered together to witness her baptism in the pool (usually covered over) situated in the Baptistery behind the rails at the front of the chapel. The water had been heated to a warm temperature and Margaret assisted by two lady members of the chapel was submerged and baptised by the Rev Jane Powell. It was moving to witness the ceremony taking place and after years of being a member of the Congregational Church, Margaret was now a Baptist.

John and Margaret Kerridge after Baptism service at Steep Lane chapel. 5th September 2010.

Brownies: "Handing over the Scroll"

The "Handing over of the Scroll" photographs were taken to celebrate the 40th Anniversary of the Girl Guide movement formed in 1910. Princess Margaret had started the scroll's journey off around Great Britain.
The first picture is taken outside St Peter's Infants School, Sowerby.
The other picture is taken along Wharf Street in Sowerby Bridge, and features Coun. Harry Haigh when he was chairman of Sowerby Bridge Council. He was also Postmaster at Sowerby Post Office for twenty-five years from 1934 to 1959.

"Passing on the Scroll" – *Evening Courier* cutting dated Wed 10th July 1950.

"The Message Goes On"
The Girl Guide Good Will scroll passed through the Calder Valley today on its way to Oxford.

Betty Cleave took the scroll by cycle and car to Sowerby village, passing it to Hazel Parkin of Sowerby Congregational Brownies, standing in the newly decorated cart. With her companions Hazel drove in the horse drawn cart to Wharf Street where the scroll again changed hands.

By pony, scooter, trek-cart and roller skates, Girl Guides passed on the Good Will Scroll. Through Halifax to Warley St John's, Bermondsey House Brownies, King Cross Methodist Guides onto St Jude's.

The scroll passed around Great Britain was to celebrate the 40th Anniversary of the Guiding movement which began in 1910.

Margaret Kerridge with the 1st Sowerby Congregational Brownie Pack – c.1961.

Brownies, July 1951
Out for a walk on the tops!

*Rear, L-R, Irene Bruce, Hazel Parkin, Carol Austin, Maralyn Parkes, Jacqueline Murrell.
Middle row: Christine Brooke, Jackie Austin, Jose Austin.
Front row: Valerie Dennis, Hilary Bagshaw, Beryl Waddington.*

*Rear, L-R: Hazel Parkin, Carol Austin, Maralyn Parkes, Jaqueline Murrell.
Front, Valerie Dennis, Christine Brooke, Jackie Austin, Jose Austin*

Guides, Old Green Chapel c. 1955
Rear, L-R: Sylvia Whitehead, Kathy Greaves, Brenda Kerridge, Ruth Handyside (vicar's daughter)
Front, L-R: Ann Lane, Joan Bottomley (behind) Norma Whitehead, Carol Austin, Pat Dixon.

Upper Field House Farm, Triangle

Upper Field House Farm, Triangle back left; foreground, rear view of a block of four cottages, now demolished. Date unknown

Farm (top left) with detached house where cottages used to be, March 2009

L-R, Rita Murphy (and her dog), Dorothy Moore, Peter Moore

Haymaking time at the Farm – atop the hay Peter Moore, L-:, ?, Dorothy Moore, Audrey Moore, John Kerridge

Sitting Pretty: On left Audrey with Dorothy

Audrey on left and Dorothy sitting on a flat backed wagon parked in the yard at the bottom of Rooley Lane, Sowerby, c.1946

The Moore family have lived at Upper Field House Farm, Triangle for over eighty years. I knew Audrey, the eldest daughter, who was born in May 1935 and died in December 2005, her sister Dorothy who was born in October 1936 and Eric born in May 1940, from attending Sunday School at the "Old Green Chapel" at Well Head, Sowerby. Peter is the eldest brother: he was born on 29th December 1930 and he and his family still occupy the farm buildings at the present time. Peter married Dorothy Whitworth at Moor End Congregational Chapel, Mount Tabor in 1961. They had four children: John, David, Stephen and Sally.

Dorothy, Mrs Lucy Winifred (Winnie) Moore & Eric at the seaside, c.1948/9

Peter's parents were called Ernest Moore and Lucy Winifred Moore (Riley) they were born in 1900, and lived at Upper Field House Farm. When they moved into the property they had oil lamps for light and very few home comforts. Peter at the age of 14 started to help his father on the milk round. He continued with the help of his wife to deliver milk from their dairy farm for over 50 years, delivering to the Pellon and Queen's Road area of Halifax. Peter retired at the age of 65 in 1995 when he sold off his milk round. The farm and approx. 44 acres of land had been bought by the Moore family during 1964, after the death of Mr George Stansfeld of Field House. Some of the rented properties were then available to purchase by tenants. When the rent for the farm was collected, the tenants would report any repairs to the property that needed attention; dry-stone walling repairs were the responsibility of the tenant!

Several local folk were employed on the estate at Field House; Harry Cawood, a next-door neighbour of Peter's, was employed as a Groom/Butler. Arthur Simpson, who lived at King Street when I was a girl, also worked at Field House; he cared for a few Jersey cows that provided milk and cream for the household. He also churned the milk to make butter. He looked after a few pigs kept for bacon and also a dozen hens that provided the eggs. With two or three gardeners also employed to grow fruit and vegetables, the estate was almost self-sufficient. The joiner was called Joe Rawnsley, and Joe Briggs from Haigh's Buildings in Town Gate was a labourer. Tommy Hopkinson was a labourer who only had one arm. In spite of this he was able to milk cows and helped out at haymaking time with this task!

The buildings at Upper Field House Farm have changed over time and the two sections are from varying dates. Alterations have taken place over the years and the property now consists of four through houses, occupied by Peter, his children and their families.

Today John breeds sheep and David raises cattle for beef production. The fields belonging to the farm have always looked lush and in a good condition; when I asked Peter what the secret was, he told me that an old farmer had said to him, "Your living comes out of the land, so make sure you look after it;" in other words, "you reap what you sow". Peter has never been away on a holiday; after they were married the couple had a touring holiday honeymoon in Scotland.

Dorothy Moore recalls her mother Winnie attending a sewing class, which was held in the old Church Institute building opposite the Co-op in Sowerby, set back from the main road. Dorothy and Eric used to go there when they had finished school lessons to wait for the ladies' class to end and to meet their mother. Miss Whiteley the teacher would not allow them into the room or to make a sound while waiting! Audrey and Dorothy both had lined coats made with brown velvet buttons, only to be worn for attending Sunday school at Old Green.

Dorothy married David Booth, who was born in 1935 and came from West End, Halifax, during September 1958 at Old Green Congregational Chapel, Sowerby. They went to live in Middlesex, London for five years, leaving for a new life in Adelaide during 1963. They had two girls at the time, one aged three and a baby of seven months; during 1964 a son was born.

PETER MOORE of Sowerby aged 80 years died peacefully on the 2nd October 2011 at Calderdale Royal Hospital after a short illness.

In Loving Memory of

Peter Moore

Upper Field House Farm, Triangle, March 2009

The Old Hall, 1630, with adjoining Field House, 1749, Upper Field House Lane, Triangle

Christine Mark was born in Halifax on October 23rd 1946, an only child; her parents were both thirty-eight when she was born. Her father, Fred Mark, and his wife, Jessie Riley, lived in Warley Road and later Stanley Road. Her father was an electrician and was in business called C.V. Terry & Co., Electrical - Engineers and Contractors, Trimmingham Quarries, Bubworth Grove, West End, Halifax.

Her granddad James ran a greengrocer's shop at the end of Raglan Street in Halifax. Her mum's older sister was called Lucy Winifred; she was always known as Winnie. When she was a baby, her cousin Dorothy used to take her out in her pram. Later, as a young child, the family would visit their relations at Upper Field House Farm for weekends and holidays. They stayed in a large shed near the farm situated in the corner of one of their fields. It had been furnished in a basic way by Fred Mark to use as a chalet for sleepovers. An Elsan toilet was also provided within the shed; entry to it was gained by another external door. As a youngster, Christine spent idyllic holidays here, out in the fresh air enjoying the sunshine in the fields among the animals. Picking buttercups and daisies and to quote Christine, "Such simple pleasures". Visits to the small plantation across the road above the Field House estate with the farm dog Lassie are recalled with affection, Christine even wrote a little book entitled "The Rabbit Wood" about the place! She used to be almost able to touch them!

When Peter had completed his milk round, Christine, when she was older, would some days walk from her home to meet him at the Dairy on Queen's Road to come back to the farm and to spend the afternoon in the countryside.

Christine has kindly allowed me to copy some of the delightful photographs from her childhood days spent on the farm. As a small child she appears to be perfectly at ease sitting with the cows, even in the days when they were not de-horned. Some had names including Buttercup and Daisy, Christine loves cows to this day!

When he was a lad Fred Mark would play out with Shirley Crabtree ("Big Daddy") and his brother Brian (a wrestling referee). Christine's other Granddad, who died before she was born, used to be a "human scarecrow". The job entailed running up and down the fields in which the crops were growing, flapping and waving his arms around to scare off the rooks and crows!

From the early 1950s: 1. Milking time at Upper Field House Farm; 2. Feeding time for the pigs; 3. Sitting among the cows and hens; 4/5 No fear of the cows – even with horns! 6 Sitting on the carthorse, held by Eric Moore

Pitts Farm: Arthur Henry James King
Born 1915 – Died 4 November 1999.

Arthur King with his new wife Imogen came to settle "Up on the Tops" in 1945.

Pitts Farm, Cragg Vale, c. 2001

When he was a boy Mr King left Harrogate to come and live at King Cross, near Halifax. In later years he moved south where he met his future wife Imogen, they were married in London. A decision was made after the war to relocate back to this area and become farmers – without any experience of living off the land. They were warned that it was "a tough country" before they departed!

They settled on the Sowerby hillside at Pitts Farm. The family eventually consisted of eight children, Randolph, Malcolm, Daphne (now known as Diane), then came a gap of five years, next was Veronica (known as Boo) and Teresa, Ignatius (now called Ian), Angela and Yvonne. Mrs Imogen King told me (January 2010 aged 89 and living in Cragg Vale) that she had always wanted to have a large family.

Copy of final details re purchase of Salt Pie Farm by my father 6th November 1944

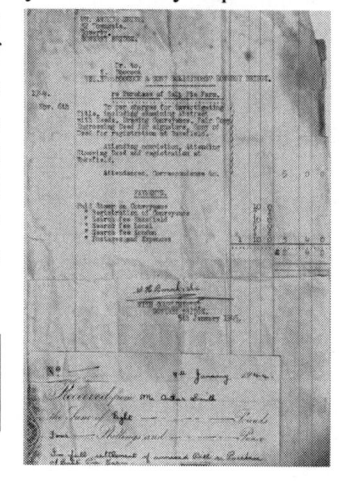

My late father, also called Arthur, befriended the couple, and later sold Salt Pie Farm and some land to them, which he had purchased in November 1944. Salt Pie was situated nearby to Pitts on the eastern slope of Crow Hill and features on a map surveyed in 1848-50 and published on the 20th March 1854. The document shows my father's bill for the search costs re- Purchase of Salt Pie Farm. It was unclear how many acres of land were included in the sale. Malcolm King has recalled that at one time 3 acres of land at the top of Salt Pie's 13 acres was ploughed one April to grow a further crop of Kale!

The building was semi-derelict and had been used for cattle belonging to my father. These would be cattle raised for beef during the days of food shortages and the Black Market as it was known then.

Mr King haymaking at Pitts

The couple had nothing much to start their life here with and the prospect ahead of them was a hard and often bleak one. It took years of dedication and sheer hard graft to turn Pitts Farm into a going concern with a dairy herd, and some beef calves for rearing. Land was bought or rented over the years, and hay and silage produced from the 87 acres he ended up with. During 1958-9 he reclaimed 30 acres of unused land: he "tamed" the land to produce hay and silage. He could produce up to 80 tonnes in a good season. His home-built silo was a large one for storage; it was 70 tonnes and 14 foot wide. It was built with the help of Randolph, then aged 15, and Malcolm, aged 13. One good summer they managed a second crop of hay; it was ready for carting away when a whirlwind blew up suddenly, lifted the lot of it and scattered it all over the moor.

He managed to grow oats, wheat and barley on the land, unusual crops in this area and at such a high altitude, although corn needed more sunshine to grow successfully. The milking arrangements were also brought up to T.T. standards. His 16 milking cows were of mixed breeds; one of his beef calves at 48 hours old weighed 114lbs, something of a record Mr King wondered? They had a carthorse at one time, which was gored by a bull, and a serious event when Mr King was tossed by a bull – he was walking with a bull pole attached to the ring in the animal's nose. The bull started to resist the farmer, and a struggle ensued between him and the bull. Having great strength in the neck and shoulders, the bull tossed Mr King high into the air and as a result he landed flat on his back! He was lucky not to sustain any physical injury although the mental shock to his system stayed with him for some time.

Mr King with his 1949 series 1 Land Rover.

As a young girl, my memories of Mr King are vague, seeing him only occasionally down in Sowerby village, perhaps at the Post Office. He was a strong-looking man of medium build and sported a large gingerish moustache; he was usually dressed in a tartan check workshirt and corduroy trousers. His wife was tall and slim with a good head of fairish hair. Sometimes they would drive down through the village in their big black Austin Vanden Plas causing heads to turn, as the vehicle appeared to cruise down through Town Gate. The children loved to ride in this car with its leather seats and walnut dashboard. The vehicle was quite a luxury for the family. It had been purchased with high mileage on the clock, so perhaps Mr King had been able to buy it at a bargain price?

As youngsters the children were educated at St Patrick's Church at Bolton Brow where Father Roddy had set up a school; they were taught by an order of unpaid teaching nuns called the Irish Sisters of Charity. This school had opened about 1953 and had around 80 pupils. They moved the school when the new Sacred Heart Catholic Primary School, Sowerby, at the bottom of St Peter's Avenue, was opened in September 1963 by the Bishop of Leeds. The school had the capacity to cater for 280 children between the ages of 4-11 years of age. Some of the King children later went on to be educated at a Catholic Grammar School out of the area; the King children were all clever or "brainy" as we used to say.

Another memory is of being told that on their large dining table there was a rotating wooden item that held all the usual condiments and additives required at mealtimes. This was no doubt a labour-saving device for a large family (a Lazy Susan?).

The Great Blizzard ---- February 3rd 1947
(As re-written from memoirs by Arthur H.J. King, Halifax Evening Courier, Feb. 1972).

We experienced our worst spell of winter weather for 30 years recently; snow fell before Christmas 2009 and lasted into the third week of January 2010. There were shortages of salt which meant that no gritting of our side roads was carried out by Calderdale Council. This resulted in several weeks of having to cope with the snow and black ice; it was a difficult time for everyone. Folk living out in the more remote hamlets and villages were cut off for days – some even weeks.

We also had a freezing winter when just after Christmas 1962 it started snowing; it was March before it finally disappeared from the Pennines. The heavy snow falls and strong winds and temperatures below freezing meant conditions were difficult. The result was chaos on the roads, Halifax town centre became gridlocked with traffic diverted from higher routes (the M62 motorway had not yet been built). Schools closed and bus services were cancelled; also building work ceased. Farmers struggled to look after their animals and the price of vegetables increased. It was the first time in history that a Football League club, our local Halifax Town, had opened up their pitch at the Shay for the public to enjoy ice-skating on the frozen ground. They held sessions during afternoons and evenings for skating and charged adults 2s 6d (12p) children 1s 6d (8p) and spectators 1s (5p).

It was so cold that even the canal froze over and regulars at the Commercial pub decided after closing time one Sunday lunchtime that they would have a game of footy on the frozen canal.

Photographs of this event published in the *Evening Courier* were taken by chemist Raymond Lumb; his shop was near the pub on Wharf Street. He was also the grandfather of my daughter-in-law Jane.

The thaw set in around the end of February; the Hebden Bridge to Keighley road was finally opened during March.

Nothing about these times of inconvenience will compare to the terrible ordeal and struggle for life to continue, as experienced by the King family during the winter of 1947, recorded as the worst in living memory.

Locals had warned that there was going to be a "great snow" coming – the ground was frozen solid and a cruel bitter easterly wind blowing. As the snow began to fall it looked innocent enough, then it became clear that this was indeed going to be as predicted, snowflakes building up and accumulating where later massive drifts would form. This was just the beginning of the nightmare that lay ahead for Mr and Mrs King with their two young sons Randolph aged twenty-one months and baby Malcolm who was eight weeks old.

The snow continued all day and at midnight the blizzard increased its force. It became clear that a rough time lay ahead for the farmer, his family and his stock. Inside the farmhouse the small fire made little impression against the freezing cold air that blasted the stonework of the building. Pitts Farm standing exposed to the elements at 1,150 feet above sea level had taken the full force of the blizzard, leaving them completely cut off in this white silent world.

Without a supply of gas, electricity, telephone or a cooking range, the conditions they were now in were drastic. No piped water was available, plus the lack of a tractor or any other farm machinery, without a horse or a sledge to utilise, meant the situation was indeed bleak for the King family. The postman did make efforts to do his round and let people have some contact with the outside world. He must have walked on the wall tops and struggled to the remote farms, risking injury in the terrible conditions. The radio run on batteries was also another source of contact and information about the world outside for the family.

The financial state of the farmer was not good and they lived a Spartan existence before the onslaught of this harsh challenge. Owing money to the bank, Mr King was relying on his heifers and cows to provide for their future. They were existing hand to mouth, therefore the larder held no reserve or back-up for the bleak time ahead. No fodder in store for the animals, no reserve of coal, fuel, bottled gas and paraffin. In later years Mr King recalled their predicament as something of a "Pennine Pearl Harbour" situation. The nine weeks that followed resembling a crash course in survival.

Opening the door on February 4th, he was confronted by a changed world: the coal shed had disappeared and only a small part of the cowshed door was visible. The blizzard was still blowing as the farmer ventured to feed his stock. The water supply came from a small stone trough in the corner of the yard. There was a hand-operated semi-rotary pump connected by a pipe underneath the cobbles. The pump lifted the flow to an overhead 80-gallon tank with the overflow dropping down into a large concrete tank where water for the cattle was supplied. Pipes were frozen inside and out: boiling water would be needed to thaw these out, and plenty of it! Temperatures were down in the 20s Fahrenheit.

Watering the cattle became a huge task as a beast can drink from eight to twenty of gallons of water a day and prefers crystal-clear water. Imagine drawing water from the well by lick pail in freezing conditions and attending to all the stock. The cows disliked the ice and snow that fell into the water in the buckets. The water system remained icebound until early April. The snow and freezing weather continued for another three weeks, snow crept into buildings, even inside drifts formed as the snow entered through the roof tiles. Standing at the top of the drive it was clear to Mr King that they were completely cut off, with no hope of any transport getting through from either end; huge drifts had formed all along the top road.

Milk

The stockpiling of milk began by filling the churns, followed by any object that would hold liquid being brought into use. Tins, bowls, jugs, Peggy tubs, any spare lickpails, were scrubbed and scalded out to be filled with the milk. This was going to be hopefully their income in the weeks to come. The 80-gallon water tank was taken down, and into the disused water trough the milk was poured. Mr King had decided that none of this precious milk from his first cows he had owned would be wasted.

The first week of the blizzard ended and the farmer was now physically exhausted by the energy spent in coping with their daily existence. He had managed a couple of trips down into Sowerby Village to pick up essential supplies for the family. The problem of the transportation of his milk to Halifax Dairies on Queens Road, Halifax was another challenge to face. Snow-shovellers were attempting to clear the road from the Sowerby end and at the Mytholmroyd diggers were also at work. Their attempts were in vain, for as soon as any progress was made, the blizzard, which continued without a lull those first three weeks, filled the cleared sections in once again. The men had then to start all over again. The prospect of any wheeled vehicles getting through was bleak, so the farmer began to build sledges for his milk to be shuttled down to a collection point in Sowerby village. There was a distance of two miles to be covered to reach the wagon. Three attempts at making a sledge that would do the job failed, each trip was abandoned as the sled became bogged down and stuck in the deep snow. Mr King was helped with this challenge by his friend Maurice Gelder who was an ex-soldier.

He had over twenty years of experience and had served in the Himalayan foothills and Afghanistan. His nearest neighbour Albert Greenwood was also on hand to assist with the milk churns on the sledge. It took them from breakfast to mid-day to drag it for one third of a mile; they had to give in when the sled stuck at the top of a snowdrift. Every trial had to be abandoned due to the masses of powdered snow. There were now six churns that were one third of a mile nearer the collection point, gradually freezing into blocks of ice.

The hard labour at the farm continued, mucking out and watering the animals and shifting the muck, all carried out in the terrible conditions. Within the farmhouse the two young children, totally unaware of the fury of the blizzard, slept soundly. Washed

Mr King in heavy snow at Pitts farm, 1970s

clothing and nappies drying in front of the fire made the atmosphere damp and steamy, absorbing the heat from the coal fire.

The danger of becoming disorientated and in keeping one's bearings whilst battling with the huge drifts was great; no pylons or telephone poles as a guide line. So easy to become exhausted and just sink down wearily into the mounds of snow could have been fatal. The words from Scott's last expedition ran through Mr King's mind, "To strive, to seek, to find and not to yield." These words helped daily as he worked and battled with the elements, sometimes so weary he would fall onto his bed fully clothed and go to sleep.

Problem Solved

It was after one night of sleeping fully clothed that the solution to the problem of transporting the milk churns was solved. It was decided to seal the lids of the churns with muslin, tie the lids across from handle to handle; drive wedges beneath the string, like battening down a ship's hatch, and drag the churns on their bellies through the snow. Corn sacks would be cut into strips, knotted together and passed through the handles with enough length left to be hauled across the shoulder. Thankfully this worked and contact with the milk wagon was made some two miles from the farm.

Two empties were brought back along with any supplies bought down in the village being packed into a large rucksack. The stockpile of milk was slowly reduced.

Occasionally the farmer was now able to hitch a lift by a van or truck and reach the dairy on Queen's Road. Comments by the staff working on the delivery platform as his churns were opened were many, as an improvised scraper had to be used to chip away the milk from the side of the cans. Then out shot something that resembled white coal slack!

The constant two-mile treks to the village for provisions and the daily struggle were taking their toll on Mr King. His joints and body ached from strain and the sheer effort of coping with his ordeal. Also because of being wet through and frozen, then later thawing out, he had developed chilblains, two rows of them on his toes and heels. These later split open causing severe discomfort and more pain to endure. As he became more exhausted, the milk yield began to drop, milkings becoming further apart. The cows were only being fed a subsistence ration of food. As a result one morning as Mr King wearily crawled back into the farmhouse at about 2-30 am, he realised he was now was only capable of doing one milking each day. Before long he was even stretched to keep up with doing even that!

During one of his battling treks on the milk haul, head down and eyes stinging and feeling engulfed by the cruel blast of snow whipping all around him, he was suddenly confronted by another person trudging the trail through the drifts. The pair silently stood and stared at each other for some time without uttering a word. Asked by Mr King how the other man's family were his one-word reply was "rough"; and the state of his cattle? His response was "Like a row o'damned kippers stood on edge! But what about thine?" "Like two rows o'damned kippers!" Mr King replied, for he had twice as many cattle as the man. Deciding to exchange notes when the long ordeal of the blizzards was over, they each went their separate ways. The sack ropes cut into his shoulders as he carried his supplies; Mr King sent up a prayer for himself and countless others who were ensconced in this cruel white world for some relief in this life-or-death struggle. Many who were elderly or sick may have perished and many financially ruined before the weather became milder.

All the fuel for the fire had to be hauled up the trail apart from sleepers that had been cut; the farm house interior was never much above freezing. What should have been a cosy room was instead, with the windows thickly glazed in ice, dark and cavern-like. The kitchen had been added onto the building as a lean-to: this became frozen from its foundations to the roof. Gradually it was being prised away from the main block of masonry. The wind pierced the rotten exposed mortar; the top course of slates were then separated from the adjoining wall. Little protection now from the storm as the flimsy inner door was the only barrier between them and the intense cold outside. (Later after the thaw, this lean-to was resurrected and shored up again after a deep pit was dug and heavy crossing sleepers sunk into the excavations.) The thaw came gradually aiding this work and the kitchen settled back, reducing any risk of a collapse.

Diggers from the Cragg Vale end had opened up the road 13 times, only for it to be filled in again. Sheep farmers were seeking lost animals daily. Not only locally, the Northern uplands were included in searching the gullies and drifts. Losses were huge and the bodies of dead sheep were still being found during June when the haymaking season began. Mr King had a friend over at Queensbury and when a death occurred in the family, the coffin had to hauled by tractor and trailer to the cemetery. In the Skipton area further north where remote farms may have an approach road of one to three miles in length, small planes were dropping desperately-needed bales of straw and hay. Black topstones were laid out in circles to show where these provisions could be dropped off by the planes for the desperate farmers and their stock.

Some weeks after the blizzard began there had been talk of a super giant snowplough that was to be brought over from Leeds to assist in the clearing of the snow. These rumours circulated for weeks and spirits kept high by the thoughts of its eventual arrival. Alas the machine was dogged by faults and developed engine trouble, the tracks broke and a driving shaft was severed. Next the rumour was that the giant blade couplings had snapped, later developing electrical problems and the most amusing story was that it kept getting, "bogged down" and was still in Leeds being inspected by "the experts". It was a superior plough to any in use and it was eagerly awaited by locals; sadly it remained just a story and it never appeared doing the job it was made for, clearing snow.

It finally arrived on the back of a giant lorry, eight weeks and four days after February 3rd, after the last shovel of snow had been cleared by the men digging 48 hours earlier! "Where are you taking that article?" Mr King inquired of the driver as he negotiated the deep snow cuttings past their farm. "Back to Leeds," was his reply, "for an overhaul" He added, leaning out of the cab, "It never were any bloody good."

Mr King had been a very fit man before this ordeal of nature during the winter of 1947. He was strong and had cycled some years earlier across the Arctic Circle by bicycle with 70 pounds of kit. He had 200 pounds of body weight and was able to break six-inch nails in his hands. The countless trail runs had taken their toll on him over the weeks he stuck it out; behind the unwashed face, this bearded man had bowed shoulders and a staggered gait. His strength had almost been completely sapped from him.

The month of March continued for the first ten days with the same fury, and then very slowly the temperature began to rise. Short spells of sunshine made little impact on the hard-packed trail, at night-time freezing once again. Around this time, help came to the farmer in the guise of Cyril Greenwood, a 17-year-old and a ten-and-a-half stone stripling. He was tired of feeling hemmed in, working in a railway signal cabin, and inquired if there was a vacancy for a farmer's man? Mr King inquired if he could shove a barrow load of muck and snow through ice and snow. After a demonstration Cyril was set on immediately. This was the start of a life long friendship between the two men. This young man's willingness to work hard combined with his strength to do so was the basis for renewed hope as they worked together as a team.

They were able to move two full churns of milk together, although the milk yield by now had dropped. The route taken now had fewer detours through the fields; after a run down they were going over drifts, inching the load over the top in a series of jerks. Some of these snowdrifts were huge: Cyril christened one the "BBB". Beyond the Travellers Rest Pub, round the second bend and opposite the end cottage up the left bank, the withered stumps of a row of old elderberry trees expose their remains. At that time they were about six feet high above the four-foot wall, and as Mr King and Cyril crossed over the summit of the "BBB" drift, the tops of these trees were well below their feet!

When the thaw did set in and the sun was strong enough to melt the deep drifts, the trails became difficult: slipping and sliding were hazards as the men carried large bales of straw on their backs from a neighbouring farm.

Snow, 1970s: Mr King on cleared road to Pitts Farm

They were tied with wire and usually weighed about 45 lbs to 55lbs; one of the bales was huge and tipped the scales at 148lbs. Slowly patches of green grass were visible and patches of roads were exposed. Drifts were sinking and the farmer and his friend now with their shovels went through the drifts rather than over them. It was while they were digging at the base of "BBB", the final blockage before access to reach the village below, that the digger from the Cragg Vale end met them. This was the first wheeled vehicle they had seen in eight weeks and two days; the plough demolished the drift in minutes.

Lower down the road at the Steep Lane crossroads lay a carcass of a dead cow. It had been dragged to there some time earlier to await collection by the knacker wagon. As they passed by a small dog emerged from out of the beast's belly, its teeth biting into the entrails. Many rotting carcases of calves, cows and stirks were collected in a big clean-up. Losses were great.

This was the scene right across the Pennines. The cattle at Pitts Farm were still standing — just! It was into the summer before their ribs were covered with flesh again. During nine weeks the milk yield had dropped from 26 gallons daily to three and a half gallons, but no cows perished. Mr King and his family were now facing ruination financially. The State helped out with some compensation, for the farmers who had lost stock and the Lord Mayor of London opened up a fund to provide help.

Snow lay around as late as April at the roadsides. During the first week in June a visit to a farm was carried out by Mr H. H. Jagger who was the District Advisory Officer of the local area of the West Riding War Agricultural Executive Committee. With a party from the Ministry in Harrogate he was visiting a farm beyond Cliviger and Portsmouth where land is about 1,400 above sea level. They were bogged down in the snow and were forced to turn back and approach the farm from another direction.

Without a doubt the winter of 1947 was the worst one to endure, although many of the old-timers told farmer King they thought that it was, "Middlin' rough!"

Trees: Arthur King - Silviculturist

Arthur King had a passion for trees and he was keen to plant many on his land. Yet again he was told that it would be a difficult task for them to grow and thrive at the farm's altitude. He was given some seedlings by Albert Greenwood; they had been pulled up from between the lines on the railway track down in the valley. These were loosely packed into a blue paper sugar bag and taken home to Pitts Farm. He knew the farmer had a love of trees, so his seedlings were the very beginning of a garden which would contain eventually over 30 varieties of hardwood and softwood trees.

The farmer's interest in trees went back to a bicycle journey that took him through Scandinavia, up the Gulf of Bothnia around the gulf beyond the

Arctic Circle, returning through Finland, Estonia, Latvia, Poland and Germany. There were trees even on the Polar rim, and throughout his 5,000 mile journey trees were his companion. They provided shelter from the noonday heat and beneath them at night he would sleep on leaves and fir needles, awakening in the morning to the song of birds. He vowed that he would surround any future home with many trees. He wrote a book, *Awheel to the Arctic*, about his remarkable journey.

Seedlings did grow and thrive and with continued plantings some 1,500 seedling and saplings were now establishing themselves at Pitts Farm. "You are beyond the tree line up here," he was reminded by the sceptics; still undeterred and remembering the birch and fir trees on the fringe of Lapland he continued to plant more. As his children grew up and left home they would return with gifts of seeds or a small sapling, pleasing their father. Sycamores seemed to thrive well and endured the snow, rain and gales that blew across the Pennines. Other varieties included larches, firs, spruces, Scots pine, poplars, beech, birch, oak, ash, mountain ash, hawthorn and elder were planted.

Mr King still planting trees at 80 years of age in 1995.

A willow tree that had been dug up from a tip during 1945 later measured 45 inches round the bole. The younger children climb the branches without the risk of them breaking beneath their weight. Silviculturists recommend that to have a healthy balance between animal and plant life about 10% of our land should be forested. Mr King also noticed an increase in the bird population at Pitts Farm and was even woken by a lark as early as 3am one morning. The struggle to establish the growth of his seedlings, constantly uprooted by wind and gales, resulted in the trees that still thrive there today: when the King family arrived, not one tree grew there. His dream was to see the Pennine slopes also planted with pine and spruce trees, possible to do over some thousands of acres of neglected land, provided labour and finance were available to do the planting. Mr King relished his hobby of tree planting and seeing the growth of the specimens over his years farming, toiling and surviving with his family at Pitts farm, Cragg Vale.

Letter to Arthur Smith, 31st January 1980
When a patient in Crossley Ward at Halifax Royal Infirmary.

Pitts Farm,
Cragg Vale,
Hebden Bridge.
31/01/80

Dear Arthur,

This is just a short note to wish you well and to tell you that we are all thinking about you and praying for a speedy restoration to health and vigour.

Your indomitable spirit and superb optimism have always been a wonderful inspiration to us all, so it came as rather a shock to see you looking shattered on Sunday, but believe me it made me feel good to think that of all your many friends you should take the trouble to look me up. Imogen was moved by your courage in the face of so many ailments.

However, remember Arthur, many a fighter has gone many rounds taking heavy punishment and then staged a recovery late in the contest and finished up the winner!

I want you to make a speedy recovery not only because you are an inseparable part of this district but I want to have many long talks with you about the good old days and your many experiences hereabouts. For that would prove an invaluable help to me in writing my memoirs.

Turvin Edge, as you know, is ground into my system, and I am beginning to feel kind of settled in, in fact the locals are beginning to realise that I am here to stay, and within the next 50 years I guess they may accept me as one of themselves!

You know Arthur, you have done many things in your lifetime, trading and deals without number, but I want to tell you that the one deal that you did brought more happiness and satisfaction than any you ever did for anyone was when you sold us Salt Pie, and knowing as you did that I was, to use a local term, "flat on my arse", waited patiently for me to pay up – that was the act of a real white man and a Christian, and I guess it was something I shall never forget. Thank you Arthur a thousand times for letting us have Salt Pie Farm, and you may be interested to know that we have now cleared all the mortgages on all the properties and have got the deeds safely stacked away, and believe me they make fascinating reading, going back as they do a 100 years or more. So now we can call all 116 acres our own, and when we have finished planting trees (I've already planted about 6,000) it is going to be well worth a look round when they are all in leaf, and in that respect we are looking forward to seeing you, but of course you don't need to wait until they are in full leaf, you are welcome at any time.

I do hope you will try and think up anything you think may be of interest to me in writing my memoirs – such things for instance as Samson Stonier holding up the bus and traffic from Steep Lane into Sowerby and refusing to reverse for the bus driver, or that iron hard-man Donkey Robinson sobbing like a child when I helped you kill his pig, or what you said to him when he asked what you thought about his deal in buying Soft Cake with 6 acres for £85, and I'll never forget your typical Yorkshire reply when you told him that he'd paid just £20 too much! Doesn't that sound staggering in the light of present property values!

So please Arthur think up all the things about the past 35 years and help jog my memory, for between us we know some fascinating stuff.

Ernest (Donkey) Robinson at Collon Bob Farm, Cragg Vale. Friend and neighbour of the King family.

When I come in next week I'm going to tell the hospital and … specialists they have a valuable specimen in the form of Arthur Smith, something unique and irreplaceable and I want them to get to work and rebuild him like he was.

Take every care and do as the nurses tell you even if their medicine is a bit nasty. I had a long talk on the phone with Ann tonight and she gave me an encouraging report about your spirits, she is a wonderful girl and you are fortunate to have such a friend. So look after yourself till I get along and don't forget to tell them to lay out the red carpet for that is the least they can do for a King.

Every Good Wish,
Arthur H.J. King.

P.S. Do give a ring if there is anything you would like us to bring in.

The letter was typewritten with a hand written signature and P.S.

Sadly the joint stories of the Two Arthurs was never to be written!

* * * * * * *

My first contact with a member of the King family came about when we had some insurance with the Liverpool Victoria during the 1970s and '80s and for a while Veronica known as Boo (King) came to our house in Pinfold Lane to collect our payments. We had never met her before but after chatting discovered who she was. When my mother died on the day before her 79th birthday, 15th January 1992, I asked Veronica to let her mother and father know. I received the following letter from Mr and Mrs King:

Pitts Farm,
Cragg Vale.
Hebden Bridge,
Hx7 5TX
22/1/92

Dear Jean,

My daughter Veronica rang me on Friday telling me of your dear mother's passing and with a request from you that we should be informed. Naturally we were distressed at the news, not only for the sake of you and David but remembering that your parents were two of the very first local residents we met on the first day of our arrival almost 48 years ago.

Thanks to your father and his extreme generosity we were able to buy Salt Pie farm in front of our own and his trust in us and help in the following years will always be remembered. What can we say except that we share your sorrow, for almost all the good folk we met in those early days of struggle and hardship have now passed on.

Do let us know if we can ever do anything for you in return and feel free to look in if you are ever passing, by the end of May things are looking at their best with the many trees we have planted over the years in full leaf.

Very Sincerely,
Arthur and Imogen.

The letter was typewritten and the signatures hand written.

* * * * * * * *

Obituary – Mr Arthur Henry James King –
as printed in the Halifax Evening Courier, *26/11/99*

Pioneering hill farmer Mr Arthur Henry James King has died aged 84.

Mr King, of Cragg Vale, was also a mechanic, explorer, artist and ecologist.

> *A walk in the snow with a canine friend! and below, Mr King with Brutus the Rottweiler pup.*

Even at the age of 84, he was planting trees and he transformed overgrown, seldom-used paths into woodland trails. Mr King, originally from Harrogate, was also a writer and produced many articles for the "Evening Courier".

In July 1938 he set off on an amazing solo journey on a bicycle costing 30 shillings (£1-50) from Harrogate to the Arctic Circle.

On his 5,000 mile trip he went from Goole on a steamer to Hamburg, then on to Denmark, Norway, Sweden , over the Arctic Circle, through Finland, Estonia, Latvia, Lithuania, East Prussia, Berlin, Holland, Belgium and back to Harrogate.

When he returned he wrote a book "A Wheel to the Arctic Circle" which was printed in July 1940. He then went to London and met his wife Imogen. They were married by Lord Soper in 1943. The couple moved to Halifax, where Mr King promised Imogen she would meet some of the friendliest people in the country.

In February 1944, he dropped his business making and painting moulded clay artefacts and he and his wife began growing their own food and battling the elements.

They had eight children.

He began planting trees and caring for trees in the mid '50s and it became his hobby in the '60s. His dream was to recreate lost forests. He worked for 52 years with only one holiday.

He leaves his wife, children, Randolph, Malcolm, Diane, Veronica, Teresa, Ian, Angela and Yvonne.24 grandchildren and 5 great grandchildren.

Ian King

Veronica, known as Boo, was born in 1957; her brother Ignatius, now called Ian, was born in 1953. He changed his name by deed poll to a shorter and easier name. I first contacted Mrs Imogen King who lives in Cragg Vale since leaving Pitts Farm. She gave me Veronica's telephone number who then gave me Ian's e-mail details.

He has his own business, "Aaron Beam Centre", which he runs from his farm, Aaron Hill Farm, Cragg Vale, Hebden Bridge, and also premises in Dundas Street, King Cross. He works with anything connected with wood, restoration work, doors and floors, etc. He is also a poet and a songwriter although he cannot read music or play an instrument! In any spare time that is available he is writing a book about the Cragg Vale Coiners.

He built his self-sufficient farm up above the Travellers Rest pub and right on the border where the Hebden Bridge area begins for postal addresses. Ian believes his farm may possibly be the last traditional hill farm in England.

This was done without any planning permission or the involvement of an architect. He spent seven years working on *Shedrock*, which was his first album, and travelled 30,000 miles to the Philippines to meet his pen-friend, Melanie, whom he brought back to live with him and is now his wife and mother to Aaron, April and Aiden.

Calderdale Council served an Enforcement notice on him regarding his habitat, to stop using "a shed" as a dwelling. Ian applied for a public inquiry and won his established rights. The story attracted the media and the story was featured on radio and reported in newspapers, gaining much publicity along the way.

His older brothers had grown up and left Pitts Farm, leaving Ian at home with his sisters. He grew up developing an appreciation and respect for the countryside, preferring the "natural" way of farming, avoiding chemicals and pesticides that can cause destruction to nature and the wildlife of the terrain. His father was somewhat old-fashioned in his farming outlook when it came to using "modern" machinery. When the Ferguson 35 tractor stood idle in need of repairs, the pair toiled and laboured manually, using a wheelbarrow that had been purchased and was to replace the work of the tractor. Ian pleaded with his father to get it repaired: this fell on deaf ears, thus entailing more physical hard graft. As a child he had no normal toys or a television to watch: the tractor was his toy!

By the time Ian was eight years old he could dry stone wall, the skill of rack of eye and being able not to pick the same stone up twice. He was his father's righthand man, and according to his father, "the only true farmer in the family". The young lad dreamed of a day when he would have a farm and land of his own to tend.

The kitchen at Pitts Farm housed an Aga cooker which was fed by the supply of sawn-up logs and old beams. Ian and his nine-year-old sister could between them operate a two-man saw; this joint effort was looked on with surprise by folk who observed them at work. From an early age the children were taught skills by their father on the farm from which they would in later life benefit. The outside tub toilet facility had to be manually emptied. This necessary task was carried out by Ian and his father, depositing the contents in a hole that had been prepared and dug out by Ian earlier. As the pair of them carried the full tub to the hole the tub would be lopsided as the youngster was shorter that his father, as a result some of the contents were deposited into Ian's Wellington boots! – the boots requiring a regular swill out in the well!

Friends occasionally came to visit the children at the farm, when they experienced a "step back in time" on these occasions, helping out in the field where traditional methods were used at haymaking time – hand raking and turning the cut grass until dry and ready for the bailer to be used. When Ian left school he worked on the farm full time.

During the '50s the task of planting the trees took over at Pitts Farm, seeds and saplings were brought in from nurseries all over the country to be raised and then planted out. The farmer was aiming to have more trees and cut back on the livestock: the aim was to "Replenish the wooded hills of Old England!"

In the mid-'60s a new Ferguson tractor was purchased, a hydraulic tipper trailer, Ferguson plough and a tractor-mounted finger-mower, bringing some modernisation in the farm's working implements. Mr King still preferred the old labour-intensive methods, at one time even relishing having to milk the cows by hand when the milking machine broke down. When the electric pump broke down, he bought a hand pump and hours were spent daily pumping water for the farm and family. It appears that Mr King preferred human sweat and bodily toil to be used in carrying out the challenges that his dreams and hopes involved for the farm.

When Ian was 18 years old, his father sold him some land; he then started his own business which he hoped would finance his own farm. Reaching 19, he bought a Ferguson 35 tractor with a front-end loader, he now began to do contract work involving drystone walling and land drains. He grew crops on his land and planted trees around where the farm would eventually be sited. He also made a road across the field, to the amusement of passers-by who wondered where the road was leading to!

With his knowledge of spring water and drains he was able to dig and find a supply for his future farm.

In 1980 he bought materials from Sowerby United Reformed Church ("Old Green") that was being demolished to build his farm. The electricity supply was installed by Ian: when he received an estimate for the installation, he realised he could do the job himself and save a considerable amount of his hard-earned money.

When Pitts Farm was sold and the building demolished Ian purchased the beams and timber from the property. The remnants of his former home were special to him, they held childhood memories and were of a sentimental nature to him.

Pitts Farm was bought by Jimmy Moore and the site rebuilt with a large modern residence and outbuildings.

* * * * * * * *

Hilda McCormack – Memories – Pitts Farm

During January 2011 I received a phone call from Veronica (Boo) King to tell me that her mother Imogen had died peacefully on the 31st December 2010 at her home in Cragg Vale, aged 90 years old. Her family had been with her at her bedside and in Boo's own words, they (her children) "sang her to heaven" with Christmas carols! The funeral was to take place on Friday 7th January 2011 at 2.30 pm at St John's in the Wilderness, Cragg Vale.

It turned out to be one of the snowiest mornings we had experienced this winter and we had some doubts about getting to the service. By the time we left Sowerby however the main road to Cragg Vale via Burnley Road was clear. We decided to park our car on the road and walk down the steep road to the church. The snow had created beautiful scenery: the whole setting was quite breathtaking!

The church soon filled up and I was taken by surprise when a lady who I first met when I was working on a checkout in Tesco, Market Street, Halifax about six years ago joined us in the pew. Later I discovered that she had worked at Pitts Farm helping on the land, the following are some of her recollections of that time.

Hilda McCormack was born in Scarborough in 1938. From about seven years of age she had already decided that she would eventually like to work with cows! During the September half-term, known as "Tatie Picking Holiday", Hilda worked along with other children in the fields at the farm where her father was employed.

When Hilda left school she was going to attend Studley College in Warwickshire as a farm student. Her father insisted that she should gain qualifications and the paperwork to confirm it. He had at one time been refused a passage to travel and work in New Zealand due to the lack of the required documentation.

Hilda's mother replied to an advertisement in *The Farmers' Weekly* and informed her that she would be leaving school the following week.

She was kitted out with the necessary clothing for the job at The Army and Navy Stores in York. Arrangements were made for her to travel by bus to Halifax via Leeds.

She began to work at Pitts Farm from 29th June to 23rd December 1955; her accommodation was a wooden shed which was known as "the shack". It had a window and inside there was a bed, a table and chair and some drawers, basic requirements for Hilda. The shed was unlined and in frosty weather a waterproof cover was needed on her bed to prevent condensation from dripping onto it! At other times her dwelling was quite cosy.

Hilda McCormack at the door of her "residence" at Pitts Farm – The Shack

Her work routine included the milking, feeding and mucking out of the cows and feeding the calves, delivering milk to neighbours on the tops, pumping water, hay-making, dry stone walling and ditch-digging, also some gardening which sounds quite relaxing after the list of hard physical jobs there were to do! One of her first jobs with the help of the children was to weed the garden: this proved a hard task as it had been neglected and was overrun with weeds. Hilda was paid 10/- (50p) a week for her labour and board and lodgings. She ate meals with the family but has little recollection of meals only that she acquired a taste for fried butter beans! (Mr King had a female farm helper prior to Hilda and also employed another one when she left Pitts Farm.)

During the summer months single-decker buses ran "Countryside Tours", some of which drove past Pitts Farm. On one occasion when the bus was passing the farm Mr King (to show off his strength) hoisted Hilda horizontally high above his head – no doubt causing much amusement to the bus passengers!

The year of 1955 was a bad one for the farmer: there was a drought when the water supply ran out from the spring. Churns were taken to Salt Pie and filled from the spring there. Eventually that also dried up and the dairy on King Cross brought them churns full of water to keep going! One of the cows died with T.B. and another was lost giving birth to twins.

The children who were there at this time were Randolph, Malcolm, Daphne and Veronica. Mrs King gave birth to Teresa on the 4th November 1955.

Arthur King asked Hilda to call him "Samson" as he was proud of his strength – he would find the "hard way" to do tasks, thinking this was the way to build and increase bodily strength! During 1955 a row of poplar trees were planted inside the boundary wall at the farm; scarcely a tree to be seen elsewhere!

When Hilda left the farm at Christmas 1955, Mr King gave her his camera, the first one she had ever owned or used: it was the one that he had taken with him on his journey to the Arctic Circle!

The Fox Family

We moved to 6 Church Terrace, Pinfold Lane, Sowerby during 1973. Mr Sam Fox and Mrs Alice (known as Trixie) Fox were our next-door neighbours at one side in the block of three houses. We were neighbours for 14 years; they bought the Curatage in 1959 – previously they had rented the property from the Rawson family – and sold it in 1987 when they moved to Pye Nest.

Their house was called "The Curatage". I had known it since being a child; their three children were older than me and had long since left home when we moved in with our son James aged four years old. The children were called Sam, Gavin and Josephine. As the boys were older I didn't really know them, although I can remember seeing Josephine standing at the bus stop below the Church Stile Pub waiting for the Tuel Lane single-decker bus to take her to Sowerby Bridge Grammar School on Albert Road, Sowerby Bridge. She wore a navy school gabardine raincoat and on her head she wore a navy bowler-type hat with a blue and white ribbon around the crown. Her fair hair was tied back into two thick plaits tied with navy ribbon.

The Curatage, Pinfold Lane, Sowerby, 20 Dec 2010 – The Curatage with porch; No.s 6 & 7, Church Terrace complete the block.

Sam and his family live in Wimborne, Dorset and have lived there for over 40 years. Gavin lives in Rockcliffe by Dalbeattie, Dumfries and Galloway and Josephine on the Isle of Skye.

Sam Fox

The following are Sam's memories as written by him.

Notes On Sowerby Memories

Fox family: Father Samuel (Sam) W. Fox; Mother: (Trixie) Fox; Me, Sam Fox born 5.9.1934; Gavin Fox born 8.10.1935; Josephine Fox, born 12.12.1938.

Mr Meadowcroft and his horsedrawn greengrocer's shop. Mother buying from him including bananas. During the war, sister Josephine was teased because Gavin and I knew what bananas were and she didn't.

Outbreak of war and war memories: Sunday morning 3rd September 1939. Mother doing the ironing with the wireless on. Chamberlain's announcement and mother quietly weeping. Her favourite cousin and other relatives had been killed in the First World War.

Starting school: started at Sowerby New Road Infants School. Mother used to take me to the bus stop and ask the big girls who went to the adjoining Secondary School to make sure I got off at the right stop. Arriving at school feeling excited because I had travelled on a camouflaged bus! In the playground one day and a heavy aircraft went over. Miss Bates, a teacher, remarking that her brother was flying in such machines. I have always wondered if he survived, the chances were hideously against him.

I remember the funeral of Norman Corlett from next door at 6 Church Terrace. Norman was a young chap who had joined the Navy. He served on board the cruiser H.M.S. Penelope. He died of an illness; I think that it was maybe pneumonia, common with sailors in ships in wartime conditions. I was in our kitchen when the coffin went past our window. In the end house, 7 Church Terrace, lived Mr. and Mrs. Hanson with their daughter Hilda. She worked at Avro's shadow aircraft factory at Yeaden: this factory built 8,000 Ansons, 300 Lancasters and several Yorks and Lincolns. In the morning a bus would collect Hilda around 6am and take her to work. I am not sure what time she returned home but it must have been a long day for her.

A sound I can still hear in my head is the early morning clatter of clogs on the setts as the people from the village who worked in the mills in the valley bottom went to work.

Running errands for mother: even at the age of eight or so we ran errands for our mother. She would give me a list of what she needed together with our ration books, if appropriate, and I would go Pinfold Lane /Queen Street to the Co-op in Town Gate and present myself at the great counter! The list was handed over and the items piled on the counter in front of me. There was a bacon-slicer, and cheese came from a great chunk with the amount you needed cut from it. When paying we gave our shareholder's number which was written onto a ticket: our number was 1981.

If mother wanted fresh vegetables I would go up to Percy Stott's allotment, which was one of a number of allotments situated behind the old Post Office. Percy loved to tell yarns and he told me stories of ships, etc.: perhaps these stories stirred an interest in ships and shipping which has stayed with me all my life. It would be interesting to know Percy Stott's background. He seemed quite old but lively to me, mind you, to an eight-plus-year-old anybody past 25 is ancient.

I remember the joiner's workshop close by the cobbler's shop in Town Gate above Castle Hill. Alec Smith was the joiner and undertaker there; he used to spare the time to talk to me as I was interested in making things. Many years later he built a garage for my father: wood was carried down the fields and passed over the field/back garden wall to be erected. When I was sent up to buy fish and chips from the shop below Providence Chapel, they were wrapped up in newspaper, mother insisted that I take our own *Manchester Guardian* for our order to be carried home in!

On Saturday I would sometimes go to the butcher to get our meat ration. I don't know why but my mother liked the one situated in Beechwood Co-op rather than up in Sowerby Village. Sweets were rationed so we used to have cough sweets called "Owd Toms" from the wooden hut situated in Sowerby New Road; these were not rationed!

Father took the car engine apart and the bits were stowed away in a kitchen cupboard. Percy Crowther at Beechwood garage had the job of putting it together at the end of the war. I think Percy Crowther must have been an air raid warden as we used to take our gas masks to him for checking to see if they were still serviceable. Early in the war he bought a Rudge auto-bike from Cyril Sands' shop on Wharf Street, Sowerby Bridge. He used to travel all over. With the bike he bought a great black leather coat.

Father was in the Home Guard and kept his rifle and other equipment in a big drawer in the kitchen.

Sunday morning walks with father
Though I was baptised at St. Peter's we weren't churchgoers and father would take us for a walk whilst mother cooked the Sunday dinner. A favourite was to go down to the railway and watch the trains. There were water troughs so that the engines could replenish the water in their tenders. Quite spectacular as the tender often overflowed. There was a huge tank for topping up the troughs and the water was treated so that it was a pink colour. During the war great troop trains of twenty-four or more coaches would struggle up the valley. Most of the goods traffic was coal from Lancashire and the empties going back again. Trains would rattle the windows of the Curatage.

Onto the canal where we would sometimes catch sticklebacks and take them home in jam jars. They never seemed to live for very long. The canal was notorious as the place where unwanted puppies or kittens were put into a sack and drowned. Other walks would take us onto the moors via Steep Lane or Hubberton.

Before the war I can just remember trams at Sowerby Bridge. During the late 1930s Halifax was getting rid of the trams and I can remember the tramlines being dug up from King Cross down into Halifax. All metalwork such as park railings, etc. was taken for scrap to help the war effort. In an open space by the Odeon Cinema would often appear items associated with national savings campaigns. On one occasion I remember the fuselage from a Lancaster bomber. In Halifax on one occasion there was a shot down German fighter.

Air raids and aerial activity
There was a huge amount of air activity throughout the war. Most was probably associated with the many bomber airfields in Yorkshire. A few memories include the time a Lancaster flew at a very low level down the valley. You could see on top of it and the noise, for that time, was tremendous. Later on I came to think that it might have been one of the dambusters practising low-level flying in the poor visibility of an industrial area. Laying in bed one Saturday night the room was suddenly lit up for a minute or so by a tremendous white light. Our Sunday morning walk was along the footpath from the village above the plantation that used to be on the village side of Field House. At the plantation a group of uniformed men were carrying a parachute. I guess an aircraft had dropped a parachute flare in order to try and see where he was.

Manchester always seemed to be taking a hammering from the Luftwaffe and the bombers would come from the east across Halifax. The sirens would go and we would go into the cellar which we used as an air raid shelter. The machines would fly over making the distinctive room-room-room sound; the All Clear would eventually sound, incident over. The siren was located by St. Peter's Church. It was then said that the Luftwaffe were bombing a town a night. Well I remember the night that it was Halifax's turn. Mother tells the story of how the night before the *Courier* had published an article on 'what to do with incendiary bombs', the answer being to cover them with a dustbin lid. On the night that the Germans visited Halifax father was away travelling in Lancashire. The alert sounded and for some reason mother put us children under the heavy dining room table rather than down in the cellar. She stood at the door overlooking the valley and King Cross. The pathfinders showered the area with incendiary bombs which twinkled over the area. No fires were started and within a few moments the lights had gone. Mother reckoned that everybody had been busy putting their dustbin lids over the bombs. The back-up aircraft circled around – the sound is in my head to this day – but then went off somewhere else as no raid developed. I think that there was a dummy town laid out at Flint reservoir and maybe the Germans bombed that. It was a dry reservoir which later on we would visit on our bikes.

Our home had a stirrup-pump, bucket and a bag of sand as I suspect all homes did. Basic fire-fighting equipment. As part of the film programme in cinemas, there were films showing you how to use these items.

On the whole I thought that the war was a very boring period. There are two further events that I clearly remember:

The night of D-Day. Lying in bed the sound of aircraft filled the air. The sound went on and on. There had never before been so much activity. We all knew that eventually there would be an invasion of Europe and with so many aircraft being around for so long it could only mean one thing. The next morning the news was on the wireless and we prayed.

The other event was Hitler's Christmas present for 1944. On Christmas Eve the sirens went and we went into the cellar, except father who stood at the door and looked out over the valley. We hadn't experienced any Luftwaffe activity for years and thought that this was probably a false alarm. We heard a sound unlike anything we had heard before. It was like a very loud raucous, slow revving two-stroke engine. Gavin and I knew the identity of every aircraft by its sound and we were yelling to father to come into the cellar as it was a doodlebug. It came right over the house and then the engine stopped so we knew that it was on the way down. Soon there was a tremendous bang and everything shook, though there was no damage. The following morning we went for our customary walk whilst mum prepared the Christmas dinner, which was based on one of Kerridge's geese. On the road from Hubberton to Cotton Stones we saw a group of people in a field further up the hill so we went to join them

I have studied more carefully Google maps, satellite mode, and come to the following conclusion. Of course it is all based on a ten-year-old's memory of sixty-six years ago. Go onto Google maps, satellite mode, and home in on the road from Hubberton to Cotton Stones. You then go up Kennel Lane where there is a farm on the right hand side just before reaching Poverty Lane. If you enlarge the view and look in the corner of a field about one to two hundred yards from the farm, on the Hubberton side, you can see a definite crater. The layout of these elements matches my memory though it would be truly remarkable if, after all these years, this is the crater made by the doodlebug. It does fit in with my memory that windows were broken in Cotton Stones, which is quite near, but I didn't hear of damage in Hubberton.

The doodlebug had fallen in the corner of a field creating an extensive crater. After all, it carried a ton of high explosive. The farm at the other end of the field must have been damaged but what I remember is a number of women plucking some geese which had been killed. It was all quite exciting and we collected some of the many bits of metal which were lying around and took them home as souvenirs. The only damage was some broken windows in Cotton Stones and an old lady died of delayed shock several months later. The doodlebug had been launched from an aircraft which had carried it to the Yorkshire coast. The object once more was to clobber poor old Manchester and I believe that one did actually get that far.

Greenwood's farm, etc.
The farm was a dairy farm and the only crop I can remember being grown was hay, which was cattle feed for the winter. However, during the war, farms were expected to grow other crops and somebody decided that the land was suitable for growing oats. As a result two or maybe three fields on the lower slopes were sown with oats. I can't remember how many years this went on for. With the exception of horse-drawn machinery, the farm wasn't mechanised, power being provided by a large brown horse called Brittain; their next horse was a light grey

one called Bob. When Gavin and I were around ten or twelve years old we, with other village children, would go into the fields at haymaking time and try and be useful. Colin Jowett from a very early age had made up his mind that the farming life was for him and I seem to remember that among the children he took a major part in the activity. We always returned home absolutely black. Several hundred tons of soot fell on every square mile every year in the pre-smokeless zone era. On the moors the sheep were black and only by travelling up into the Dales did we see white sheep.

Milk was delivered by one of the farm workers whose name I can't remember. He would come down the field with a yoke around his neck and a churn hanging on either end. With this lot he would climb over the wall, come down the steps from the back garden and start his round at Church Terrace. Milk was ladled out using measuring cylinders with handles that hooked over the side of the churn.

Later Dennis Greenwood delivered milk by horse and cart carrying the milk churns. This horse was Bob; the yellow painted cart was stored under an open shed at the far end of the yard at Stile Farm situated at the rear of the Church Stile pub. A great innovation was the first tractor, a grey Massey Ferguson.

The farm updated its preparation of milk by installing plant to pasteurise the milk. I think that father was involved in planning the installation due to his experience with boilers, calorifiers, etc.

An event was when the cows which were kept inside during the winter were let out to graze when the weather got warmer. They would race around, jumping up and down and then eventually settle to somewhat more sedate behaviour.

Winter

We always got snow in winter. A horse-drawn snowplough and men with shovels would keep the roads clear.

One Christmas day, somewhere around 1943 I think, there was a sledge in the front room with our presents piled onto it. It had been made by the pattern makers at Hartley and Sugden's where Dad worked. A great feature which we discovered later was that the runners were from half round steel strip. When going down some of the longest runs this made it one of the fastest sledges in the village. Sledging was a great social event among the village youngsters. Our first efforts were down Queen Street, but when we were older we moved onto Upper Field House Lane. We never sledged down the fields. I think that the road provided a faster more exciting run. After tea we would meet at our favourite run, down Upper Field House Lane as far as Dean Lane, and spend the whole evening repeatedly racing down the road and trudging up again. Of course the road was turned into an icy slide to the consternation of the adults but I don't remember any notice being taken of their protests. We just considered them to be spoilsports. That sledge was used winter after winter and must rank as one of the most "fun things" we ever had.

The winter of 1947 was memorable as many of the roads higher up the hill were filled to the top of the walls with snow. The men couldn't clear them sufficient for vehicles but would shovel out narrow passages so that it was possible to walk along them.

Winters could be vicious. On one occasion a young chap crossed a field from his home to the Traveller's Rest, above Steep Lane, for a social evening. When he came to return home a blizzard was raging and they didn't find his body until the snow melted. [And this ties in with Mr King from Pitts Farm. Mrs Fox had decided to call at Collon Bob Farm beyond Pitts on the day the "great snow" came: Sam had "fallen for a girl who lived there". Trixie was going to visit and give the young lady "the once over". The blizzard had begun as she left the farm. Seeing a lady in a dangerous situation Mr King approached Mrs Fox and guided her through the driving snow to the top of Steep Lane where she was able to continue her walk in less severe conditions back down into Sowerby and to reach home safely!]

Post War Memories

In 1946 Gavin and I were given bicycles for our birthday presents. Most of the other 'gang' also had bikes and it became a favourite pastime to race around all over the place making a nuisance of ourselves. The speedway came to Halifax and we used to emulate the riders by sliding around the school playground. One day I slid over the wall with the bike on top of me, creating a gash above my eye. Mum banned cycling but we were hooked on it and so the ban didn't last for long. I can't remember that it altered my behaviour but the skills gained proved valuable many years later.

Sam (R) and Gavin on their bicycles Pinfold Lane, 1946

In the late forties the new council estate started to be built, with the first houses being the pre-fabricated Tarren Houses. It was at this time that the village was officially vandalised by having one side of the street demolished. This was done bit by bit when a new road opposite the Co-op was built onto the estate. One building of a row had been gutted and one day we were playing in it. We had just moved out when there was a loud 'crack' and the wall fell across the road with the rest of the building ending up a heap of broken stone. A massive cloud of dust rolled down the street towards the church. Part of the adjacent house had been pulled away and a very upset irate little old lady had a chunk of her bedroom wall pulled away.

"A Winter Walk along Dean Lane and Mill Bank" 1947

1. Dean Lane with Bluebell Wood on the right. 2. Sam (13), Jo (9), Gavin (12) walking uphill with Sheila the family pet. The row of six cottages at Nether-ends in the background was demolished in the '60s. 3. Rear wall of Gatelands barn. 4. Deep snow and drifts Left – Sam, Jo and Gavin. 5. View From Mill Bank showing the graveyard and Norland beyond.

Fires
I can remember two fires whilst living in Sowerby. The first one was at Row Lane Farm. Where there is now what looks to be a block of three garages used to be a barn full of hay. It caught fire and by the time the fire brigade arrived the place was virtually gutted. Quite a crowd gathered. I think that the building was damaged to the extent that the roof fell in.

The other fire was at St. Peter's School. I think that the headmaster must have lived next to the school. Anyway, he had a garage where he kept his car. One day the car caught fire in the garage. I didn't see the fire, only its result.

Flood
We often got heavy rains and the rivers and stream would react by rapidly filling up. It was quite common for the Calder to flood but there was space for the water to spread out. On one occasion in the 1940s, Wharf Street in Sowerby Bridge was flooded. The only time I know that this happened.

On another occasion the little stream through Cotton Stones became a raging torrent. At the junction of Lumb Lane and Alma Lane there is a row of cottages. Half were washed away together with a woman living there. On a Sunday walk we went round to view the devastation. Apart from the wrecked cottage the road was torn up, total devastation.

By the early 1950s our first bikes had been sold and Gavin and I bought from Cyril Sands of Wharf Street, Sowerby Bridge (now Deli-Beli) more sophisticated machines. We joined the CTC and on Sundays travelled vast distances throughout Yorkshire and adjacent counties. We would travel down the hills at tremendous speeds. If there was a westerly gale blowing we would struggle over the moors to Blackstone Edge – then with the wind behind us run off the moors into Ripponden, often passing cars on the way, such was our speed. Going down Sowerby New Road into Sowerby Bridge, or down any of the hills could be a fraught experience. The roads had a tarmac strip down the middle which was fine. However, at the sides the surface was made up of stone setts which gave a very severe shaking if you met a vehicle coming the other way and had to go onto them. These setts were kept there so that the horses got a grip with their feet, which they apparently didn't get on the tarmac.

Money for my bike came from summer jobs. From the age of sixteen I went from Sowerby Bridge Boys Secondary Modern School on a County Continuation Scholarship to Halifax Technical College. We had long summer holidays and I spent most of the time earning money working at local firms. The jobs were varied but in 1954 I worked on the houses that were now being built further up the hill in Sowerby. On my first day I was taken by the foreman along a muddy track of a road to where a line of house bases had been built. As the site was on a hillside the bases were needed to provide a level floor for the building. The foreman showed me a number of long planks, a wheelbarrow, a shovel and a mound of rubble. I was to use these implements to get the rubble into the base and fill it up. The first few hours were spent acquiring the skills needed to make plank walkways and manoeuvre a loaded wheelbarrow along the planks, tipping the load into the right spot. After numerous occasions dragging the barrow from the bottom of the pit I eventually got quite good at the job and in the next few weeks filled the bases of several houses. The problem was the weather as when it rained, which was often, we sheltered in the wooden shack and I didn't get paid. Eventually I left and went to work in the packing department of Harella in Halifax.

In October of that year I joined the R.A.F. and except for visiting Mum and Dad didn't have anything to do with Sowerby afterwards.

Easter 1989. The last action involving Sowerby was after father died: we had a family and friends gathering at the top of Crow Hill in order to scatter his ashes. Crow Hill lives in the memory of daughters Susan and Caroline as one of the places most frequented when we visited and went walking. Later we also scattered some of Mum's ashes (she died aged 90 July 2nd 1998 in a nursing home in Dorset) on Crow Hill so that part of her could be with father. The remainder went to the churchyard by the sea at Newbiggin in Northumberland. She never gave up being a Northumbrian and her love of the sea, so it seemed fitting that she should maintain the connection for eternity.

Trixie Fox with Dodger at Newbiggin-by-the-Sea, Northumberland

Sam and Trixie: wedding guests

Trixie with car Teddie

Scattering Sam's ashes, Crow Hill
Sam Fox Snr died 1989. Photograph taken at Easter that year by David Green, retired Chief Photographer Halifax Evening Courier. Lifelong friend of Sam Fox Jnr and the Fox family.
L-R: Sam Fox, daughter and son-in-law --Caroline & Gwynfor Jones, Gill Fox, David Fox, Gavin Fox with partner Liz Bailey, Alice (Trixie) Fox, Mhairi Fox, Jo Fox, Phyllis and John Stainton (close family friends).

Gavin Fox

Gavin contacted the Book Case during February 2009 with some feedback about his childhood memories for me; later we exchanged e-mail addresses and he provided me with some more details. He connected with many of the people who were mentioned in my book and had his own childhood memories restored. Gavin was born on 8th October 1935. He lived in Sowerby for 28 years.

Educated at Heath Grammar School he worked at one time for Asquith's and Pratt's in Halifax. Later he worked as a contract draughtsman.

During 1966 Gavin left Sowerby to live in New Zealand; he returned to England in 1969, he then left for Australia in 1970. He moved to Sydney and was there until 1991.

After leading an adventurous life travelling the world, he is now settled in a small coastal village called Rockcliffe By Dalbeattie in Dumfries and Galloway since 1997.

Like many people he also regrets that the village was mostly demolished during the 1950s to make way for the council housing estates to be built.

Looking back he now regards this was an act of vandalism. He confesses that he may have innocently started the demolition process himself, playing one day in the derelict old farm in Town Gate opposite what was the Co-op now Town Gate Stores. Climbing out of a window opening to the rear of the building he saw a large, heavy misplaced stone tile. Slowly he pulled it out and dropped it into the field behind the building, thinking that it would make the building a safer place to play in. As he stood in the field he heard a rumble, he retreated further back into the field away from the building.

To Gavin's horror the rumble was now a roar and the huge gable end slowly toppled in to the road. Simultaneously the roof collapsed and the front of the building fell outwards scattering huge stones across the main road and onto the pavement in front of the Co-op. A huge black cloud of dust arose from the fallen masonry, eventually when blown away revealing a scene of total chaos.

The lady who resided next door to the collapsed building rushed out into the street to survey the mayhem. Looking upwards at the first floor gable end of her house, her bedroom furniture was now fully revealed, bed and all. The bedroom wall lay in a heap on the road with the other debris from the farm. "Look at me bedroom!" she shrieked in utter disbelief. Shaking like a leaf Gavin pretended he was a casual observer passing by, who had narrowly escaped being squashed to death by the collapsed building! The road must have remained blocked for hours; luckily there were no injuries, Gavin returned home quickly, before the village policeman came on the scene.

Gavin recalls the geese that belonged to Ernest Kerridge, father to Brenda, John and Margaret of Queen Street. He kept poultry in the field that he rented from Jimmy Greenwood at Town Farm. At the top end of this field stood the large hut that was used by the Sowerby Band to practise in. The field is situated backing onto Queen Street and slopes down into Pinfold Lane. Mr Kerridge would raise half a dozen geese for his friends leading up to Christmas for their dinner tables. When Mrs Trixie Fox used to walk up and down Pinfold Lane the geese would greet her with loud cackles and squawks. Little did they know that one of them was going to end up on the Foxes' dining table for a festive meal. Trixie treated them as pets and found it hard to imagine their fate.

He recalls when he was a lad of about 11 or 12 years old some time during or just after the War when the family had been using their cellars as an air raid shelter, Gavin and Sam decided to "liven things up" a little one dull afternoon and to "drop a bomb" on the local baker Mr Broadbent's old Dodge bread van as it drove down Pinfold Lane underneath their high garden wall. The "bomb" turned out to be a fair-sized stone, the lads never expected it to be a direct hit, and unfortunately it was!

There was a screech of brakes, and the boys realising the enormity of their actions hid in the garden. The Curatage at one time had fourteen trees growing in the front garden so they had a good choice of hiding places. The garden gate opened and a severe looking bread man strode up to the front porch and banged on the door. Mrs Fox answered the door and there was a heated exchange of words; he left after what seemed an eternity. The boys moved around in the trees as Mr Broadbent made his way down the path, out of the gate and back to his van. It was then that all hell let loose! The baker had made their mother ring the police whilst he stood and listened from the door. This is where her experience as an actor with the local Halifax Amateur Operatic Society came into action! She lifted the phone, dialled and spoke to a phantom policeman at the other end, which convinced the baker that the affair was now sorted and action would be taken.

Gavin's memory is somewhat blurred from that moment onwards, but their father had a mean slipper which he used with real panache for any serious breaches of behaviour.

Barry Copley was a friend of Gavin's who lived in Sowerby Hall. He became mad on motorbikes along with another friend, John Kerridge, who lived in Queen Street. The pair of them could dismantle and put a machine back together again.

The Copley family had a shed in their garden and Gavin would spend happy Saturday afternoons playing with model aeroplanes and model diesel engines.

They used to fly the planes on Grace Fields on Dean Lane, where Barry taught Gavin how to balance a bicycle. He would seat him on his bike at the top of the slope, holding him up whilst gathering speed. He realised that Barry was still near the top end of the field and he had now grasped how to ride a two-wheeler cycle. Little would Gavin realise in those childhood days just how riding a bicycle was to feature in his adventurous years that lay ahead of him!

Gavin has given lectures about his travels including four in Scotland for the Royal Geographical Society; he also speaks to local interest groups and once a year in December for the Cyclist's Touring Club at the Oddfellows Rooms in Halifax. His cycling companion was the late Eric Biddulph from Huddersfield. The pair completed some big rides together, once riding the Karakoram Highway in northern Pakistan and the Himalayas in 1991. Another trip to Spain when Gavin was 65 was to visit a memorial that had been erected in memory of Gavin's late uncle Ralph Fox who came from Halifax. They left Halifax for Portsmouth and sailed to Bilbao, arriving in Lopera on October 27th 2000 after cycling down through Spain. Gavin was proud to be going on this journey which was happening 100 years after his uncle's birth. He was also looking forward to the journey's 1,200-mile round trip. Travelling light, the only things he took on the journey was a change of clothes, a tool kit and his passport!

During their visit Gavin and Eric were shown around by the Mayor of the town. Their visit over, they next cycled down to Malaga, and flew home with the bikes to Liverpool. This journey had been a moving experience for the cyclists as they learnt a lot about the Spanish Civil War and the plight of the working classes and the humanitarian issues, which were always a concern of Eric's.

Sailing
Gavin and his brother Sam are both competent sailors and have spent a great deal of their lives afloat and navigating their boats in various oceans and waters.

Gavin built his own yacht in his spare time when he lived in Australia. He was a teenager when he first was introduced to yachting in the Lake District with his friends. He did distance sailing down the West Coast of Scotland and has also acted as crewman on a trip from Tasmania to New Zealand, where he learned hints on navigation and handling the conditions that could be experienced in areas that experienced bad weather. Gavin was also a friend of Colin Swale and his wife Rosie, a Halifax couple whose sailing adventures hit the headlines in our papers.

His yacht, a 39-foot cutter, was fitted with auxiliary power to enable tight manoeuvres to be carried out. It was named "Katafigio"; at the launching of the yacht Gavin placed a silver coin under the mast – this traditionally means good luck!

Jo Fox: Sowerby Town – Memories of a Pennine Village

I was born under a Christmas tree on December 12th 1938 in The Curatage, Sowerby, the only one of my family to be born in the village. The house stood on the edge of the village, built in Victorian times, when many new curates were being assigned to help overworked parish vicars in the Church of England.

The house stood four-square, four rooms downstairs and four up, with a draughty hall from back to front through which the winter wind whistled, and a wrought iron balustrade to the stairs and landing. My parents had modernised the house, putting in electricity, which had to be brought down from the village. There was an indoor water closet placed where the alcove in the scullery had been with a narrow passage to it where coats were hung, and a set of golf clubs I never remember my father using, and an old tennis racket I never remember my mother using, but it was the eve of a great war which would impact on everyone, and life would never be the same.

Upstairs the end of the landing had been cut off to form a narrow bathroom with a claw-footed bath and a sink. A room from which, when I was older, I would look out on wild moonlit nights and watch the clouds scudding by and the branches of the sycamore tossing against the sky like a soul in torment. Sometimes I would creep in early in the morning to watch the sunrise across the Calder Valley.

My parents had come to the house as newly-weds from my father's home in Halifax, and to keep in touch with family and friends they had one of the few phones in the village, which was sometimes used in emergencies by neighbours as there was no public phone nearby. With the electricity my mother could be a modern young wife with a large American fridge, a washing machine and electric iron, but the old copper for boiling clothes was still there in the scullery, and once became a breeding place for mice which led to a major mouse massacre. Outside, in the garden, was a large stone trough for washing clothes, another remnant of "mod cons" dating from when the house was first built. In the scullery was a white enamelled butler's sink, but so far from the cooker at the other side of the house that my mother hated it, and was so happy, when long after the war, a new stainless steel sink was plumbed into the kitchen close to the new electric cooker, so hot summers days were not made even hotter by the stove being lit for cooking. The thermostove, made at Hartley and Sugdens in Halifax where my father worked, provided hot water, heating and cooking. Another modern marvel was the futurite laid over the stone flagged floors, providing an easy clean and comfortable surface, but in the kitchen there was a reminder of earlier times when the Curate would have had servants to care for him and his family, a set of bells, the notes of the scale denoting which room attendance was required in. As children we had great fun playing the bells using a long broom handle. My mother had a maid, but she disappeared when war broke out, and I inherited her bedroom.

The two smaller houses adjoining the Curatage, forming Church Terrace, were for lesser officials of the Church: they did not have separate sculleries, but a kitchen with shallow stone sink, and this was also the living room, no separate dining room and sitting room with window seats and wooden shuttered windows like their grander neighbour, no indoor toilets and bathrooms, no electric lights, just hissing gas jets, a small front parlour overlooking a strip of garden, instead of a large garden full of trees where we played, and a porch with stone seats on which presumably in an earlier age parishioners had sat waiting to see the curate. The occupants of the smaller houses had to wash in the sink, or heat water for the tin bath. No fridge for their meat and milk but a wooden box with mesh front to allow in cool air and keep out the flies. Whatever the weather, they had to cross the strip of land at the back to the dry earth closets with the timber seats, framing the smelly black holes that led into the ashpits behind. The Curatage had its own closet, no longer used, but the ashpit was filled from all three houses. It was a large stone enclosure with a half door, and the ashes from the fires would be flung in there, and soak up the excrement from the adjoining toilets. In summertime the flies abounded, so there was a great deal of swatting went on, later replaced by long sticky fly papers which dangled from the light cords, and later by DDT, which probably poisoned us. About twice a year the ashpit men would appear, open up both doors of the pit and shovel out the contents into a cart.

Once a week our neighbours yellow-stoned the windowsills and steps of their houses, and edged them with white, and washed the pavements, not an occupation my mother indulged in. The war isolated her on the edge of a village with elderly neighbours, with whom she had little in common, and three young children who were asked to be quiet when playing so as not to disturb the older people, and to be careful when crossing the common area to keep away from their pavement on the way to the back gardens. An understandable attitude, but hard on a young mother.

The front of the house looked over the Calder Valley, with the river, canal and railway. We used to watch the long goods trains, smoke pouring from the funnels, and try to count the number and types of wagons as they crawled along the valley bottom, hoping they would stop to take on water from the large raised circular tank that stood by the track. A popular walk when I was old enough was down to the canal where we caught sticklebacks, under the bridge, and put them in a jam jar to carry home. I don't recollect they ever lived for very long, probably died of starvation.

By the canal and railway was a large mill where our friend Mr Ogden worked: working in such an imposing building added mystery and importance to his character. Near there a ford had once crossed the river, and Roman coins had been found there, maybe an offering to the Celtic river goddess in this Brigantian area. From the ford, a track had climbed the hillside, passing only a field's width from Church Terrace on its way to join the Roman Road at Blackstone Edge, the main crossing over the Pennines.

Along this track had come later travellers, Danes, who gave their name to the village, Sorby, one of the villages that grew up along the line of the millstone grit where the water poured out as springs unable to penetrate any deeper. The valley bottoms would have been swampy and full of dense forest where bears and wolves and wild boar roamed, and the almost barren hilltops were wild and wet and windy, a place where Neolithic man had hunted and lost his precious flint arrow heads. The spring-line was an area where people could establish settlements and farm, and later great herds of hardy sheep would provide the basis for the woollen industry, and the prosperity that made possible the building of large comfortable farmhouses from the fifteenth to seventeenth century, built of millstone grit, with beautiful mullioned windows, and the large halls of the wealthy landowners and merchants, such as Wood Lane Hall that lay just below our house, and fascinated me as a child.

I loved the old houses, and was sad to see so many in a ruinous state with hens in the bedrooms and the windows gone, but before this time it seems the Normans came up the track, possibly it was then that Castle Hill got its name as it would have been natural for them to put a fortification there, perhaps that was also the time of the Hell Field, where apparently the dead were buried, maybe after a battle. I understand that Sowerby became the centre of a large area stretching from Todmorden to Wakefield, a hunting forest given to the Earl of Warren, who made a Culpan steward to administer this estate.

Later, during the civil wars, more soldiers came this way, and the people of Sowerby prepared to defend themselves once more, and Culpans were still living here. The following century, in 1783, Martha Culpan was born and later married Joseph Todd Fox, a joiner, my own direct ancestors. I was glad to have been born in the village of my ancestors, and feel this ancient hillside village, founded on millstone grit, is very much a part of who I am.

Looking from the back of the house, up the hillside, above the vegetable garden, was another field bounded by the farm. Here lived Jimmy Greenwood, a person and place of great importance in my early life. From here came milk, and with the milk local news. The milk usually came round in a horse-drawn cart, in large shiny churns, and sitting inside the churns were different sized measures. Jimmy used to come into the scullery and measure out the required amount and relate to my mother the latest news from the village, then he would go to the houses next door, where the procedure was different. On the windowsills were left the jugs neatly covered by a muslin cap, maybe with a crocheted edge, and weighted by a fringe of beads to hold them in place. I was never quite sure which method had the greater status, and whether my mother would do better to follow her neighbours' example.

Sometimes one of Jimmy's assistants would come down the field and over the garden wall to deliver the milk: this always seemed more exciting, but even more special was when extra milk was needed and we would go up to the farm to collect it from the mistal, a dimly lit cave with the smell of hay and manure, warm cows, and before the days of mechanical aids, Mrs Greenwood quietly milking, and we would wait until she was ready to fill our jug with the warm milk. My memories of Mrs Greenwood are of a tired-looking woman of few words, of whom I was always a little afraid. I once saw our cat Sinbad there, with the farm cats hunting mice in the barns. This was his private life which he didn't share with me; I was completely ignored, this was not the cat who slept on my feet at night.

Bob Holland with his horse and trap outside Town Farm, Sowerby. Note the sign over the door – Bob Holland Butcher – and the meat basket in the cart. The street still had setts. Bob lived here before the Greenwoods; his slaughterhouse was later our washhouse at 32, Town Gate.

  Initially, the place of most importance to me was the garden, with its many trees, later cut down because the roots blocked the underground water course which ran, not through a pipe, but in a stone flagged drain. This subterranean world could be dimly observed through one eye pressed against a crack in a stone covering a larger chamber, partly hidden by an overhanging elderflower and surrounded in the grassy shade by milkmaids, one of the secret and charmed places of my young life, listening to the water chuckling musically underground During very heavy rains the cellar under the house would flood, and I had dreams of our own swimming pool. One exceptional year there was so much rain that springs burst out all over the hillsides, even through the surface of the roads, and new burns flowed everywhere cutting fresh channels in the soil, and our garden wall, high above the road, had waterfalls running down it, turning the lane into a river

  This part of the garden had a high retaining wall down onto Pinfold Lane from which occasional pedestrians could be observed, and passing vehicles, which led to an interesting experiment by my older brothers: was it possible to drop a stone on top of a vehicle and for it to stay on? Unfortunately the science was not appreciated and apparently my mother had to do some apologising to an irate baker.

Pinfold Lane was very much a part of my growing up. The lane was so named because of the enclosure for straying cattle just where the track branched off down to Wood Lane Hall, which led into the valley bottom: this was at the bottom of our garden. At that time the Hall was divided into a number of cottages but it was later bought by the Sugden family who restored it to its original glory, and one Christmas I had the pleasure of being there in the large central hall with its minstrels' gallery, and a decorated tree that seemed about twenty feet high, a huge log fire in the ingle nook fireplace and a number of Great Danes warming themselves by the flames, and one of the family, ladling punch from a silver bowl placed on the long refectory table, reminded me of Mr Pickwick in *The Pickwick Papers*. A truly Dickensian and memorable Christmas, particularly as I had just had four wisdom teeth hacked out, and could barely open my mouth, so my carol singing from the gallery was very muted, and the mince pies were fed in crumb by crumb.

Where the back access to our houses led into the lane, there was a gas lamp, and for those who could climb up on the field wall it was possible to get hold of the brackets that the lamplighter leaned his ladder against, and swing on them. The lamplighter was not amused, and boys would torment him by swinging there when they knew he was about to appear at the top of the road, but running away before they could be identified. Later we would watch and see the spread of electric lights across the opposite hill side, initially along the line of Burnley Road like a jewelled string.

In the summer time a fire-breathing panting monster would appear at the top of the lane, a large steamroller, and then the road would be tarred, rather a pleasant smell, but care had to be taken not to get the tar on clothes and footwear. Inevitably some did get on our skin and had to be cleansed with butter. Down the road came a giant of a man, but a very sad, thin and stooped giant. At first I was a little afraid, but later learnt he lived at Steep Lane, and was just exceptionally tall. I came to realise he must have been very lonely. Up and down the lane at different times came a horse-drawn grocery van, knife grinders and menders of pots, a cyclist festooned with onions, even a muffin man.

Looking over the wall at the side of the garden, onto the back, was a row of older cottages: originally it must have been one long house with mullioned windows, but now formed three cottages. In the middle one was an old man with a small dog and an unmarried daughter; as a boy he had lived in Heptonstall and heard tell of my great-great-uncle Joseph who had been a curate there until defrocked. According to him the vicar was jealous because of uncle Joseph's popularity: he drank beer with the men while the vicar drank port with the gentry.

Butting up to the main cottages, at right angles, was a very different cottage, possibly older, and in the corner was a small dark home, inhabited by an old woman. It had a small front room which from my recollections was used as a shop, selling a few sweets. I was always warned against going in there, and had the impression the old woman had special powers, not necessarily for good. I think the embargo did not apply as much to my brothers.

When I was older I did go round to the back of the house where there was another small but brighter room looking onto the walled garden. The older cottage had been condemned, but during the war was occupied by a family from Liverpool called Pratt. I went in it once with my mother when one of the children, Anne, was very ill; my recollection was of very low-beamed ceilings, dim lamplight, and a small glow for the fire. My mother nursed Anne through her illness and as an adult she came back to visit. Next to this cottage was an outbuilding which I think was used as a privy but apparently it had once been the local lock up, it would have been uncomfortable for even one person incarcerated there.

It was by the wall of the lane here that another drama was enacted: from recollection on a summer's afternoon, a woman from the W.V.S. appeared with a request, to me an odd one, there were a number of children needing homes, would my mother take some in? My mother's initial response was that with three young children she felt she had enough to cope with. Later the woman appeared again: it seems there were three brothers who wanted to stay together, and no one had the room to put them up. Having a larger house perhaps my mother would oblige. My mother obliged. Three boys from London moved in sleeping in one room on camp beds provided by the W.V.S. The middle one I remember as Arthur, they all went to St Peter's School during their stay, and their parents came up to see them once.

My only other recollection from that time, was their looking over the wall across the Calder Valley and saying 'Ooh, isn't Yorkshire large?' They were right, but even from Sowerby not all the county is visible; after the visual restriction of London streets it must have been a shock. They stayed about six months, and introduced us to a variety of comics. From recollection the *Beano* and *Dandy* were acceptable to my parents, others less so. I think *The Rainbow* also appeared and this was probably where I read the adventures of Rupert Bear.

The other memento from their stay was Bonnie, a Dutch rabbit, female. We already had one rabbit, Beauty a blue Bevrin; my mother acquired him when she was going for singing lessons. Her singing teacher kept Beauty in a cage in the porch and mum made friends with him; when it came time for him to supplement the meagre wartime meat ration my mother begged for his life. Beauty became my special friend, and father of Penny, Tuppence, Threepence and Fourpence. The first lot of rabbits found homes, but second time round they ended up in a pail of water. As the two rabbits were kept in separate cages, the multiplication was a bit of a mystery. I can understand my mother's reluctance to take on three more children, cooking and cleaning for eight people would not have been fun.

My entrance to the village was up what to a child seemed a very long steep hill, bounded by high stone walls that I couldn't see over, though on the right side the field rose above the wall, so I could make out Christmas dinner, in the form of a goose being fattened by Mr Kerridge Just before Christmas mum disappeared in the garage among a cloud of whirling white feathers, and Christmas dinner had talk of who got the parson's nose and who got to pull the wishbone – the person with the largest piece would have their wish come true.

One of my first memories of walking up the lane was finding a dead bird and being allowed to carry it home. I took it to the nursery and putting it on the floor tried to work out what made the difference between a dead bird and a living one, what is life and what is death. My brothers had already made drawings on the walls of aircraft and bombs dropping from them, so they must have been concerned with other thoughts of death.

When the air raid warnings went we took refuge in the cellar; my father had tried to build an Anderson shelter in the back garden but everywhere he dug there seemed to be drains, so he called in Percy Stott who, as the landlord's agent, had drawings of the drain network, and his efforts were supplemented by Mr Quain, a water diviner from Sowerby Bridge; everyone had fun with the mysterious rods but it seems there was water everywhere.

The war didn't mean a great deal to me as a child; I hated the gas masks, the air raid siren was a hideous noise, getting out of bed in the middle of the night seemed strange, shortages were something I grew up with. There was excitement when streamers of silver foil appeared dropped by planes to disrupt radar signals – I made them into 'icicles' to decorate the Christmas tree. Then there was the time small parachutes were dropped with flares to drag through the non-existent cornfields on our hillside and burn the crops, and the last Christmas when we were shaken in the cellar and mum thought maybe it was a movement along the Craven Fault line, but it was a flying bomb landing on the hillside above us, possibly destined for Manchester, or maybe it had overshot London. We walked up and retrieved twisted fragments from the crater. I kept mine for years, precursor of later, more accurate, moon landings and voyages into outer space.

As I grew taller I could see over the wall into the field where Bob the horse grazed, and hay was cut in the summer, and the cows grazed after their long winter internment. Sometimes, during the summer, the sound of a brass band would waft across the hills, and the cows would all run to the point nearest the music.

During the war we had Double Summertime to help the farmers, and I hated being sent to bed, and lying awake in broad daylight listening to sound of hay-making, longing for the time when I should be able to join in. One summer I did; I felt sorry for all the mice running from the cutter, but enjoyed feeling grown up enough to help rake the hay into rows, and turn the rows to help them dry. I actually did very little because I was quite small, but it felt good to be included. Then running behind the hay cart picking up any bits that fell during its journey up to the big barn by the farm, and getting a ride back down on the cart. In those days the hay was covered in soot from the heavy industry all around. Only during Wakes weeks did the hills behind Halifax become visible.

I was gradually growing up, but compared with my older brothers my world was still very restricted. They went off to school in Halifax, and when at home could go up to the village to play and make friends: I was still on the outside. Sometimes they would play with me in the garden, but being four years younger it was boring for them, so cowboys and Indians would leave the Indian tied to a tree in the garden still ostensibly part of the game, while the cowboys were away on adventures in the village. For me the village seemed rather remote, a place where the unexpected could happen.

At the top of Pinfold Lane was the Church Stile Inn, and behind it a large barn where swallows nested under the eaves in spring, making wonderful round nests, to me it was unbelievable that they could have flown all the way from Africa. Next to it was another barn where the bull was kept, sometimes I heard it roaring and was afraid it might break free. The pub was then kept by the Coleys, a place which could safely be entered by men, and sometimes by women if accompanied by men. One hot Sunday, on the way back from a walk up Crow Hill with Dad; he called in for some refreshment and to buy me some Dandelion & Burdock, and I waited outside with some heather I had gathered on the hill. As the men tumbled out of the pub to go home for lunch they bought the heather from me – it did make me think that possibly here was a way to augment the pocket money that had started at a penny a week, then two pence, three pence, sixpence, ninepence, one shilling, at annual increments. At the end of the war I spent a whole shilling on a small blue balloon – it was fragile magic that I had never seen before, my most precious possession.

Opposite the pub was Mr Steadman's greengrocery. From recollection this was a tiny shop and much of the produce was out on the pavement in boxes; if it had to be inside, there was scarcely room for a customer. It was here I saw my first bananas. Until then I had only known them as dried fruit, and I loved the bright yellow colour, so different to the brown of dried ones. It was here one Christmas Mum bought a box of tangerines, each wrapped in silver paper looking very exotic. In the days leading up to Christmas I got to look at them, sniff them, touch them gently, but not unwrap them. After Christmas dinner we were each given one, and at last I could slowly remove the silver paper and enjoy the brilliant orange colour, then savour the delicious juicy fruit. There was one left, and mum said she didn't really like them so the last one was divided into four and shared.

Fruit was scarce during the war, and afterwards. I had once sat during a school playtime feeling one of the privileged just to watch a child peel a blood orange, divide it into segments and share some of the precious segments with very close friends. I did half believe it was real blood in it so was happier to watch than eat. After the war boxes of apples were sent from Canada to St Peter's for the children, one each. On the way home I was followed by children begging me for the core, as I usually ate everything I felt quite like Lady Bountiful in refraining from devouring the core and letting another child have it. From recollection it was one of the Nickerson children, a family of about 16 who lived further down the lane in a large rather dilapidated house on Finkle Street, a steep road leading down into the valley.

It was in this tiny grocer's shop that I saw a pomegranate, and persuaded my mother to buy one. I thought they were a magical fruit because I had read about them in Greek legends, the fruit that Persephone ate in Hades so that when she returned to her mother Ceres, above ground, she was condemned to spend six months of the year underground because she had swallowed six seeds. It was the most disappointing fruit I have every eaten, all seed. I have tried again since, and for me it is still a mystery why anyone eats them.

Behind Mr Steadman's was a narrow alley between some cottages and the wall of the graveyard. In the graveyard was a 'house for the dead' in which bones had been put from graves that had been dug up to make way for the new church. I wasn't sure whether some macabre parties went on there with so many dead put in one place. The flags of the pathway were old gravestones, and the area seemed dank and gloomy.

In one of the dark, tiny, damp cottages with gravestones for the floors, lived Mrs Ruby Ford, the village dressmaker, and here I was measured for a dark blue taffeta party dress, so I could go to a pantomime party with the daughters of some well-to-do friends of my mother in Halifax. They had met at Halifax Light Opera Society as they both enjoyed singing and performing. I was tall for my age, and at St Peter's was called elephant, and foghorn: neither name did much for my self-esteem. Mrs Ford's words linger still in my memory, 'Don't worry Mrs Fox, she is all in proportion.' Mrs Ford later had a daughter Malan, a keen dancer, hopefully all in proportion, and they moved to one of the new Swedish Tarran houses on the new estate, for which half the village was unnecessarily destroyed.

Walking up the village, on my way to the school I attended from the age of eight – having been to Sowerby New Road Infants School for my first three years – I passed the small park which I remember from the antirrhinums, or snapdragons, planted there, I loved them. During the war the chains around the park disappeared 'to help the war effort' but some years later they reappeared.
I understood, that before the park was created, this was the site of Sowerby Town House which had been designed by my great-grandfather, an architect in Halifax. If this was true, the Town House could not have stood for long.

Sowerby Town House, demolished approx. 1933, a Council building used for meetings and a committee room by the Sowerby Local Board. It stood where the small park is situated.

    The children of Martha Culpan and Joseph Todd Fox had moved down to Sowerby Bridge, the new centre of activity in Victorian times, with the railways, and canals, the mills with first water power, then steam. One had a timber yard where the Catholic church now stands, another had a chemist shop, and in those days, before dentists, would also pull your teeth; others became involved in the woollen mills. Those of the family moving into the professions moved on to Halifax, one to become an architect: from joiner to timber merchant to architect, a movement through the generations and the towns, a distance of four miles.

    Next to the park was the village well: sometimes, in a very dry summer, houses would be without water, and women would queue at the well to collect water, I heard this well never ran dry. Our own water was from a spring and it was delicious; I have never enjoyed drinking water since. Unfortunately a newcomer to the area had it analysed and it was condemned so everyone was put on the town supply.

    Across the road were the almshouses, which I loved: they looked so pretty and unusual. They had been rebuilt by the Rawsons who owned Church Terrace. Together with the Stansfelds they were the main landowners in the area, mysterious people who seemed to inhabit another world above ours. My father paid rent for many years before being allowed to buy the house.

    The church of St Peter's stood opposite, and chiselled into the lower courses of the wall is the alphabet, an unusual feature. I used to love hearing the bells ring out on Sunday morning, or the special peals for weddings or the tolling for funerals. During the war they had been silenced but rang out for victory.

That was the day we hung the Union Jacks from the upper windows of the house, and sometime after that my mother took me down to Sowerby Bridge to watch Churchill pass along Wharf Street on his way to Rochdale. There were large crowds and we stood in Tuel Lane to try and get a good view. This was part of his campaign tour for the first elections after the war when it was assumed the hero would be elected, instead the Labour Party won with Clement Atlee as leader, and radical policies for a National Health service, new towns, and local authority housing programmes. A special petrol allowance enabled my mother to use our old car 'Matilda', a blue Ford Ten with running boards and a starting handle, to take people who were disabled to the polls.

Rationing continued for many years after the war, and it was exciting to be able to go to the Co-op for the first time and buy my first un-rationed sweets, I spent weeks deciding what to buy, but the choice was very limited when I did get there. I was in the top form when I was measured to see if I was tall enough to qualify for extra clothing coupons, I think you had to be about 5'4"

The teacher for the top form was Mr Proctor. I had a great respect for him, and it was he who introduced me to local history. I did well at school but wasn't happy; having spent my early years in Sowerby Bridge, and not being allowed to go and play in the village, I had no friends there. My life was spent on the fringe, and many of the children thought I was a foreigner. I had been very upset one day, years earlier, when I was sitting on the back step of the house, and the new local vicar passed by and stopped to chat; after which, he said knowingly, 'I can see you are not from around here.' I felt deeply insulted having been born in the house behind me, and my ancestors being from the village, but my accent was not a local one, and at school that counted against me.

Across from the school was an old building, that was empty and unused, along with many others it was torn down, my mother thought it may have been the old moot hall.

Sowerby Hall, divided into cottages, sat in the centre of the village, near the well, and was one of the houses I loved. It was near here that Mr Berry lived who walked whistling down the lane carrying his ladder when he came to redecorate the Curatage. All the striped regency style wallpaper had to be trimmed by hand, rolls and rolls of it, and my first and last lessons in decorating were from Mr Berry: I learnt how to hang paper and gloss paint. The black doors and skirtings became white, and the dark green outside paint was the start of a revolution when my mother, against all local established custom, had the doors and windows painted white. The revolution was on, a new era was beginning. The war was definitely over.

I am still a loyal customer of the Co-op, and remember those days when most of our shopping was done there. Shopping was usually accompanied by a shopping list. The assistants selected the items from the shelves, sugar was weighed into blue paper bags, and the tops neatly turned in, bacon was sliced on the machine to the required thickness, and all the parcels were carefully fitted into the shopping bag, or basket, making the best use of space, everything was an art.

Further up was the butcher's shop, which my mother used when I was a teenager. It was here I became a vegetarian: one day it was too much as bones were sawn through, kidneys and liver displayed, the great empty tunnels through the heart where blood had recently pumped. I did not want to sink my teeth into this flesh, these felt like my bones, and heart, and so I became a vegetarian, and it was three years before I met another. It was just before my baptism in Halifax Parish Church, on my sixteenth birthday, when Mrs Ogden, as my Godmother, presented me with the English prayer book inscribed with the words 'All things bright and beautiful, all creatures great and small, all things wise and wonderful, the Lord God made them all.'

Castle Hill and rear of Trinity Cottage, 2009

Continuing up the main street was another lovely old house with mullioned windows, called Castle Hill: it stood back from the pavement with a courtyard in front of it. To the right hand side, by the pavement, down one or two steps, was a tiny room with no windows that I recall. The door stood open so the cobbler could be seen bent over his work, rows of lasts on shelves around the walls. By that time few people had shoes made, and few could afford repairs – holes in soles were often filled with cardboard. As a child I looked in and thought I was looking into a fairy tale; maybe this was the cobbler who could make a pair of red shoes that would carry you dancing over the hills and far away, but the red shoes were unaffordable.

Across the road, was another magic place, the old Post Office with its beautiful porch, and dim interior lit by gas, the stone flagged floor and in the distance the thick mahogany counter presided over by a cheerful genie, Mr Haigh, an important man in the village, the man to whom I went when I needed my first passport photograph signing.

Nearby, and in gardens behind, Mr Stott presided over his empire, fresh seasonal vegetables, peas, beans, cabbage, cauliflowers etc, and under the protection of glass, cucumbers, but again the magic: to the side was a space for flowers and among them were everlasting flowers. How could real flowers be like paper and never die? I loved them and sometimes there was money for a little treat. Except on Sunday walks I normally never went further than this on the roads to Hubberton and Steep Lane.

Sowerby Post Office, c.1936. Stuart (4) and Mary Haigh (2), children of Harry (postmaster) & Connie Haigh

Going back through the village was the Rich Man's House (Haigh's Buildings), but where was the rich man? Was he hiding in an upstairs room, ready to pounce on unwary children? I realise now it could have been hundreds of years since the rich man lived there; I would like to know who he was. Behind the empty building a green field speckled with wild flowers where I made my first daisy chain, and in the field a small dell where in winter ice flowers would form on the rocks. I believe the house, dating from the thirteenth or fourteenth century, was pulled down and taken to a Museum in County Durham but has never been erected, another piece of local history lost during the fifties.

The worst winter was just after the war, when the snow was higher than the field walls, and when it melted it froze, icicles on the barns stretched down to the ground. Trees were covered with ice and when the wind blew they chimed like wind

Jo, Gavin, Sam & dog. Deep snow 1947

bells. Fuel became scarce but my parents managed to get hold of some peat, so it was still possible to cook and have hot water. Jack Frost decorated the windows at night with the most wonderful patterns of ferns, and I undressed in bed and kept my clothes beside me so they would be warm to struggle into in the morning, still under the blankets. It was great for sledging, but I cried with pain from chilblains when I came into the warmth. We sledged down Queen Street to the top of Pinfold Lane, but that winter I was told some sledged from the hilltops all the way down to the valley over the snow-covered walls.

My last winter in the village I was posting at Christmas, and my round was the top end of the village up to Hubberton and Steep Lane and back down to Boulderclough and home. I was so happy, walking on my own through the snow to all the old farmhouses and cottages that I loved, meeting the people who lived there, being out in the early morning in the silence of the countryside, on the high hills the snow curling like waves into drifts, sculptured by the wind, brilliant white against the blue sky.

There are many special moments I recall from my Pennine childhood, the shining celandines in the spring with the sunlight dancing from them in the fields off Dean Lane, the old stone cattle trough further down the field with a frog: if you kissed it would it turn into a handsome prince? Perhaps all love of place or person turns it to beauty. The small wood with the stream in which we built dams and sailed paper boats was one of my favourite places at the end of Dean Lane.

My feelings about the Curatage are mixed. My nights were filled with nightmares, and sometimes when awake strange happenings. Was the person whose breath I felt on my face real or a draught, were the curtains being drawn along the rail, when the curtains had been taken down for washing, just a mouse, or the strange entities in my bedroom one night, did they exist? Later my father also experienced them in the same room.

One incident was not imaginary, because it was shared. One Saturday afternoon I was sitting at the kitchen table doing my homework when I felt a strange chill down my back; the two dogs sat up with their hackles raised and were obviously watching something moving around the room. Another time my mother was alone in the house, by the sitting room door with the cat, Boysie, in her arms, when two ornaments on the piano were swept off onto the floor, and one, the balloon lady, broke. All the time the cat was watching something my mother couldn't see. I would be interested to know if the present occupants have encountered any mysterious happenings.

Outside the family the person closest to me during my childhood, was Mrs Ogden, sister of Jimmy Greenwood; she was my best friend. I loved going down there past Row Lane Bottom, to the little house with the ornamental brasses that were ritually cleaned on the same day every week, the beautiful china figurines and little ornaments that were in the front parlour, where I could see them as a special treat. Mrs Ogden seemed like a universal Aunt, always ready to listen and understand a child's problems, and with fascinating stories to tell, that I never quite knew whether to believe: did the garden gnomes really have a secret life? Her sister Mrs Clare lived in a new bungalow a few minutes' walk away. She always seemed a person set apart, not only because she had been disabled by polio and spent her life in a wheelchair, but because she wrote poetry and was an honorary member of the 'Hen Pecked Husbands Club' for which she wrote a new poem every year. She also had a pet owl that she had rescued as a chick, and it followed her around and perched on her shoulder. More magic for a child meeting this creature of the wild.

My only regret about my childhood is that so much of the village I loved was pulled down in the 1950s, the green fields where I played covered by a housing estate, and the lush Grace Fields, the best village pastures where Gavin taught me to ride a bike, now have a school on them, looking out to Norland and the Ladstone Rocks where Sam carved his name. The rugged rocks formed one of the boundaries of my childhood walks, a place where other stories could become a reality.

Town Gate, cleared for the new estate, 1960s. Rooley Lane Chapel and Sunday School on the left, Old Green Chapel with spire behind.

The village and immediate surroundings, the people I knew as a child, strongly influenced my growing up and the person I am today.

The gritty reality of life was all around me, the sense of history rooted in the Pennine hills, but also a wonderful magic which I hope other children still find there, but I do feel that much of the magic may have faded and mine may have been the last generation to experience it.

December was always a special time for me, the time of my birth, and the cold frosty snowy starlit nights that I loved, and the excited anticipation of Christmas day. One Christmas Eve I was snug in bed and fast asleep, when I awoke to the sound of a heavenly chorus outside my window singing "Hark the Herald Angels Sing" for a few moments I felt transported to another world, that Christ was born again and a new age of peace on earth had come, that glory shone all around. Then I realised I was in my bedroom and outside Steep Lane Baptist choir were singing.

Ralph Fox
Ralph was an ex-pupil of Heath Grammar School in Halifax and later Bradford Grammar School. At Oxford University he gained a degree in modern languages. He was a founder member of the British Communist Party in 1920 and visited China and Russia. He was also a prolific writer and a published author; his books included biographies on Genghis Khan and Lenin. Another book was set in his childhood Halifax and was called *This Was Their Youth*. At the onset of the Spanish Civil War he was one of the first volunteers with the International Brigade. The war attracted volunteers from all over the world. He was there for six weeks during some heavy fighting and was killed near the town of Lopera near Cordoba in Andalucia at the end of December in 1936. The monument erected by villagers is in the Memorial Garden there dedicated to his memory and also that of the poet John Cornford who lost his life on the same day. In September 1999 the Mayor of Lopera unveiled a memorial in memory of the two men: it is sited in the Jardin del Pilar Viego.

In 1950 a memorial seat was dedicated to his memory at Bull Green in his home town of Halifax it bears a plaque to honour Ralph Fox (incorrectly dated) and reads:

A memorial plaque to Ralph Fox ----

In tribute to the memory of
RALPH FOX
Writer Friend of the People
Soldier for Liberty
Born in Halifax 30th March 1900

Killed in action in Spain 3rd Jan 1937

IT IS SAD FOR A MAN TO DIE
WHEN HE IS SO LOVED BY THE PEOPLE

* * * * * * * *

Mike Freeman, a local Sowerby author and retired lecturer, is an admirer of Ralph Fox and has done extensive research into his life for a book he is writing about him. He rates him highly as being significant in the political and literary scene during the '30s, as a man who carried out his beliefs and dreams.

During November 2010 members of the Fox family from all over the country met at a re-dedication event in Halifax when a new memorial seat with plaque was moved to a new site at the Piece Hall. Mike Freeman presented the family with a hard copy of his book, *Ralph Fox: Telling the Times*. John and I were invited to the dedication and reception at the Imperial Crown Hotel. It was lovely to meet up with members of the Fox family after many years and to meet Mhairi (Fiona) Josephine's daughter who we had last seen as a baby!

Feedback

Small World

In my *Growing Up in Sowerby* book on page 89 there is a photograph, "'Old Green' Sunday School Anniversary – 1955". An error of mine was spotted by a reader in Adelaide, South Australia, resulting in a phone call to me from a lady in North Allerton, North Yorkshire! The girl I thought to be Sylvia Walker (second row from front, second from left) was really Christine Mark, now Capstick. Dorothy Moore who is her cousin had sent Christine a photocopy of the photograph from Adelaide. Dorothy had been sent a copy of my book by David Sutton, her brother-in-law; Audrey her sister was married to Gordon Sutton his brother. There followed a series of phone calls, e-mails and even a visit from Dorothy and her husband David when they were over here during August 2009 while they were touring and catching up with relations and friends: more surprises were to come!

As soon as my husband set eyes on Dorothy's husband David he exclaimed, "You are the image of Dougie Booth!" – a man he used to work with at James Chambers Timber Merchants, Pellon Lane, Halifax. We were all taken aback when Dougie turned out to be David's father! After several letters and e-mails between Christine in Northallerton, another coincidence arose: her father Fred Mark had also worked with my husband John at Chambers' Timber; later he had worked in his capacity as a self-employed electrician at our first home in Hampton Street, King Cross and later when we moved up to Church Terrace in Sowerby. Fred has also worked for Fielding & Bottomley of Wellington Street South, Halifax, when they carried out shop fitting work all over the country. John was employed there as driver/ handyperson. It really is a "small world".

The Traveller's Rest

The Traveller's Rest at Steep Lane has been sold (May 2011) after being vacant for some time (Aug/Sept 2010). The building, which dates from 1623, had been run by Caroline Lumley since April 2002, the restaurant becoming well-known and award-winning. It has been bought by Peter Sawrij with planning permission for conversion into two houses and to renovate an adjoining cottage with landscaping to the car park.

CONCLUSION

This collection of memories and tales contributed by folk either born in Sowerby or having a "Sowerby" connection, now reaches a conclusion. Special thanks to John Kerridge, Sam Fox and Jo Fox for their written memoirs. Also to Vera Kerridge for allowing me access to her memoir "The Dancing Years". Thanks to the people who sent me details by e-mail and by post, also to the folk I chatted to in their homes to hear their recollections.

Their fascinating tales have brought to life the hardships and the joys of living and time spent in Sowerby. It has also revealed a strong bond that "Sowerbians" feel about the place where they grew up, with contributions adding to the social history of this special place!

For more information about the history of Sowerby and photographs old and new, go to www.Sowerbytown.org.uk

APPENDIX 1: The Last "Old Green" Newsletter

SOWERBY UNITED REFORMED CHURCH

FOUNDED 1645

CLOSED

DECEMBER 2nd. 1979

Recollections.

The closure of our Church at Old Green is a very sad occasion for me, as no doubt it is for us all. My family have attended here for many years, my father, my grandfather and my great grandfather and probably more before that and of course at the present time - my immediate family and their children are connected with the Church. I look forward to the plan that I am sure that God, in His wisdom, has marked out for us, but at the same time I can't help looking back at all the happy times that we have shared in this place.

My very first recollection of the schoolroom was an "At Homes" a three day event in those days, held at Christmas, and I can see the sweet stall at that affair, full of lovely chocolate and things which could'nt have and right at the top of a stand on the stall, a row of small milk churns full of chocolate drops, how I wished I could have one but there was'nt enough money so I just had to go on looking.

I remember my first concert, I think I was Miss Muffet or Little Bo-Peep, I had a crook anyway and I was very nervous I know.

Then in Sunday School I remember lining up outside the Primary door waiting for Miss Rose Haigh to play the march for us to go into the Primary to and the lovely stories we used to listen to. There were the Sunday School Anniversaries when for weeks before we had to go into Church on Sunday afternoon to learn the hymns, we were never really keen on that but then the Anniversary day dawned and we were all dressed up in our new clothes feeling proper toffs.

The Whitsuntide treat was always a great day, we would meet at the school and process round the village and Beechwood singing hymns and the big boys at the front carrying the banner, then back we came to Sunday School for tea. We were very fortunate at Old Green, our friends at different Churches in the vicinity all had currant cakes and coffee in the field but we always had a sit down tea, a bag of sweets and an apple, then we went to a field for sports. I remember that one such field was somewhere on Dob lane then the venue was changed and we always used the cricket field for sports, races etc. I remember my sister Brenda winning a ball in a race - I did'nt win anything that year - and I was so jealous I threw that ball as far as I could down the road, needless to say I was sent to fetch it back and I got a good hiding for doing it. Then there were the Missionary plays, I remember I played the part of a small coloured girl in one of them and somewhere in the play was a storm, they had to use a sheet of tin to make the sound effects and it frightened me so much that I believe they had quite a job to get me back on to the stage again, that was in Mr.Fletcher's time and that reminds me that Mr.Fletcher once came to our house to ask me to read a passage out of the Bible, I knew what he wanted and I saw him coming, I was about 9 or 10 at the time and I did'nt want to do that little job at all, so as he approached the front door, I climbed out of our back window, he did'nt catch up with me on that occasion but he made up for it afterwards.

There was the Choir too, I remember once doing a musical play in Sunday School and Mr. Leah the choirmaster must have liked the sound of our voices and invited us to join the Church choir, we would be around the 11 to 14 age group and at that time it was quite some thing to be invited to join the choir. We had practises quite regularly and they were hard work, but Mr. Leah was a perfectionist as you all know and only the best would do, this is why we had such a good choir and this is something that I have missed. Once every year we had a Choir outing, we left home very early and always went quite a long way, breakfast, lunch and tea being provided, we really enjoyed these occasions. At one Choir practise we were learning a religious cantata called 'The Coming of the King' Mr. Leah was kneeling up on the buffet conducting when he suddenly lost his balance and fell, not only off his stool but almost into the the Choir stalls, of course none of us dared let our faces slip and we had to wait till we got outside before we dared laugh, which we did of course, being young.

Besides these memories I remember a lot of the folks who used to attend, Mr & Mrs Jack Leach, Mr & Mrs. Arthur Leach, Mr Emerson Lumb and his wife, Mr & Mrs Selwyn Lumb, and one lady who was a regular attender who without fail during the Communion service would get her purse out and rattle all the change around, I was sure that everyone in the Church would be able to hear her.

As we got older we became Sunday School teachers ourselves and was involved with Guides and Brownies and Youth Club and finally I became an Elder but my memories are so numerous they would fill a book.

I hope that those of us who are able will continue to worship elsewhere and that the years to come will have as many memories for me as 'Old Green' has had in the past.

M. Kerridge.

Dear Members & Friends.

This will be the last newsletter that I shall ever put together for our Church – no more "From my Window", no more puzzles or thought for the month, and no more articles or items from those who have contributed to the newsletter and to whom I owe my very sincere thanks. The closing of the Church seems to me to be a time when thanks are due to quite a lot of people – to all those who have ministered here from the time of its founding – to all the devout men and women who have held office here and have faithfully carried out their duties – to all the many generations of families who have worshipped here – and my own personal thanks to the present membership, who from the time when I joined them have made me feel as though I belonged. As Mr. Woodburn has remarked –"we have been like a very close family here"– and I think this is true, with the love and fellowship and a feeling for each others needs that a family has, and I feel very privileged to have been a part of it.

Yes, it is an ending, but all endings give us an opportunity for a new beginning and whatever we take up and whichever way our paths take us we will try to keep in touch and may God go with us all.

A very nice little event occurred on Wednesday of this week, it was the last occasion on which the Brownies were able to meet together as a pack and unbeknown to Margaret the Brownies had decided to mark the occasion suitably and so had the District. We thought we were just having a little get together with the mothers of the Brownies to discuss their future. When the evening commenced I must admit that we began to get a whiff of something impending, hurried whisperings in corners, disappearances from the room, mounting exitement, all pointed towards a happening of some sort, though to give them credit not one of them let a word slip though they must have been bursting to say something. It was when one or two fathers arrived with the mothers and a few division commisioners, then one or two people with cameras arrived, then a county commisioner that we knew it was going to be something special and it really was an occasion to remember. After we had all had tea and biscuits the Brownies first of all presented Margaret with a lovely Crysanthemum plant and a stainless steel dish with a picture of the Piece Hall engraved on it, and then I received the same but my dish had Shibden Hall engraved on it, they were not only from the present Brownies but from past members too. Then came the presentation from the division, this was a new award and had only been given to one other person before Margaret, it was a lovely brooch and was a silver Guide badge on a blue background, it is the county award, given to those who are retiring from the movement after long service, Margaret has been Brown Owl at Sowerby for 30 years and well deserves the award which was presented by Mrs.Hull the County commissioner. I also received another plant for helping. So even though it was a sad occasion in some respects it was a really nice evening and we both enjoyed it very much. I forgot to say that we had each received a lovely crocheted mat from some of the Brownies earlier which we much appreciated so I shall sit and eat nuts or sweets from my dish while I look at my plants which will be standing on my mat and think about them all. Margaret of course will also be able to wear her brooch and I can tell you all that she feels very proud to be able to do so.

* * * * * * * *

To all those who have been feeling under the weather we wish you all a speedy recovery, our sympathy goes to Marion Laycock and family in their very sudden and sad bereavement.

* * * * * * * *

One last very big THANK YOU to all our members and friends who have helped us with all our efforts to raise money in the past — we are now engaged on raising money for cancer research so please support us when we have our little bring and buy sales or coffeee mornings etc... may we wish you all the best for the future and a very Happy Christmas and New Year.

* * * * * * * *

- Margaret Jowett

APPENDIX 2: OLD SOWERBY

Cottages at Sowerby Green, demolished mid to late 1920s, situated opposite the graveyard wall of former "Old Green Chapel"

*Cottage, Wood Lane, below Littlewood Lane Farm.
Date of demolition unknown.*

Old postcard showing Steep Lane with Steep Lane Baptist Chapel on the left and The Manse on the right

Grace Fields opposite Field House, Dean Lane, Sowerby – an old postcard

Haugh End – an old postcard

Looking down Town Gate to St Peter's Church. Sowerby Hall on the left, the Rawson Almshouses on the right behind the railings.

St Peter's

Rev J.R. Sykes and St Peter's choir – Whitsun Walk to the Almshouses 1955/6. Adrian Paley at the rear with other choir members, Garth Kellett, Stuart Hawksworth with the cross, Berkley Stabler, Mr Parsons and Albert Schofield were also members. Note the sign for Stocks Lane on the wall in front of Sowerby Hall.

St Peter's Sunday School Pupils 1956/7 taken inside St Peter's School. L-R, Sheila Bevis (Stabler), David Shields, Tony Wilson, Allan Bruce, Roger Heap, Denise Simpson (Howe), Pauline Preston (Ray), Sandra Bull. Front, ?, Pat Allen, ?

Church Stile pub

View of Church Stile pub and Sowerby New Road. Postcard dated 1938.

Stanley and Eleanor Mount, Licensees, behind the bar at the Church Stile pub, 1970s. Long serving Landlords, 1965-1984

Stan with Coun. Austen Benbow and Prince the Alsatian outside the Church Stile pub - during the 1960s. [Evening Courier]

Vandalised Bus shelter and the small park with the Church Stile pub [Evening Courier]

*Regulars outside the Church Stile Inn 1960.
Left: ?, Les Horne (with bag), Ted Snowden, ?, Keiran Lynch;
Rear: John Madden & Terry Bottomley.*

John and Terry on park wall in Queen Street opposite pub. All these pictures were taken on the same day.

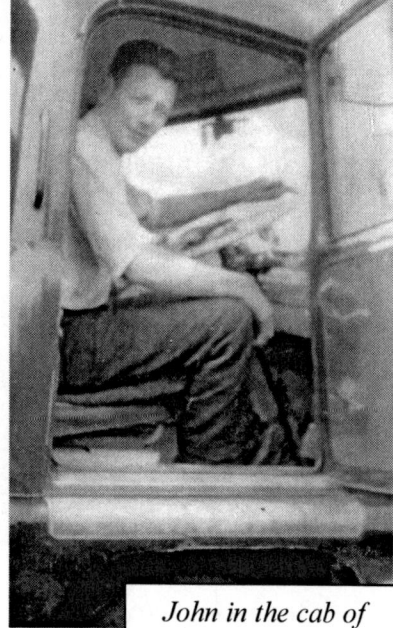

John in the cab of Collett's wagon

The landlord at this time was Stanley Fisher 1958-1961. Harriet Murphy is now the landlady.

Town Gate

Looking down Town Gate. The roof of the old fish shop is visible on the right. Date unknown.

Mother with child to the rear of the houses with archway, nos 31-45 Town Gate.

Town Gate cleared ready for the estate. Providence Chapel visible on the right, demolished in the early 1960s

Sowerby New Road

Sowerby New Road was completed in 1929. During the 1930s Pollit Avenue, part of the Beechwood estate, was built to the rear of the wall on the right.

View of Sowerby New Road and West End taken from the Norland hillside. The Methodist Church which stood on the left by the row of poplar trees in Sowerby New Road closed in March 1958. Photo taken later.

Friends and Neighbours

Pat Medlock aged 2, sitting on a Sowerby doorstep.

Sowerby Friends. Left Audrey Halstead holding baby Lynn Medlock, Pat Medlock and Mary Haigh

Blanche Riley-Gledhill (Helliwell), aged 2, sitting on a mounting block to the rear of the Star Inn, Sowerby, July 1924.

Blanche and her children looking smart in snowy Hubberton!

Blanche and Randal Helliwell dressed as "Jack and Jill" for Sowerby Gala 1924/5. Standing outside no 5, Queen Street next door to Town Farm.

Helliwell Family Group 1926/27. L-R: Blanche, Donald, mother Annie (nee Kerridge) with Hazel, Kenneth, Randal and father Edgar

The Helliwell children at Littlewood Lane Cottage, late 1920s

Park Outings

Sowerby Bridge U.D.Councillors with Park officials: inspection at Crow Wood Park, Sowerby Bridge 1965/6. L: Les Moran, Mrs Elsie Bagshaw, Michael Myers, Frank Uttley, Chief Financial Officer; Austen Benbow J.P., Leslie Godfrey, mac?, Colin Beverley (rear), George Parkin, Emma Brook, David Paley (trilby) – Parks Superintendent; Alfred Womersley (trilby), Clerk to the Council); Walter Turner? and Tom Barker (white mac).

Trentham Gardens 20th June 1947. An outing organised by headmaster of St Peter's School Mr Wright. Mother is standing in front of him and I am in a white dress at the front.

Housing

Pre-war Old People's Bungalows, Beechwood Estate

Post-war Newlands Avenue

Post War Tarren Houses, The Newlands, Sowerby. Photos from SBUDC Tenants Handbook